His father was still on the burning ship . . .

Angus pulled himself and Yellow Dog onto the red boat, which was sloshing with water. He realized, dimly, that the boat was drifting away from the *Cormorant*. But there was nothing Angus could do, even if he could have reached his father's burning ship.

Angus saw the column of orange flame writhing against the dusky sky. The *Cormorant* looked small and terribly far away.

"DAD!" Angus screamed futilely. Then the horrible sight was blotted out by a wall of water crashing it down into the sea.

Panic seized Angus. His father was gone! And he was alone, more terribly alone than he ever imagined he could be.

FAR FROM HOME

THE ADVENTURES OF YELLOW DOG

FAR FROM HOME
THE ADVENTURES OF YELLOW DOG
™

A novelization by
RON FONTES *and* JUSTINE KORMAN

Based on the screenplay by
PHILLIP BORSOS

Troll Associates

TWENTIETH CENTURY FOX Presents A PHILLIP BORSOS Film "FAR FROM HOME: THE ADVENTURES OF YELLOW DOG"
BRUCE DAVISON MIMI ROGERS JESSE BRADFORD TOM BOWER Music by JOHN SCOTT Edited by SIDNEY WOLINSKY
Production Designer MARK S. FREEBORN Director of Photography JAMES GARDNER Produced by PETER O'BRIAN Written and Directed by PHILLIP BORSOS

Special thanks to Laura Rubenstein.

CHAPTER

1

he old pickup truck bounced down the long driveway. Bright yellow leaves danced in its wake. Fir- and cedar-covered hills rose above the peaceful green valley. No green on Earth is as lush as the green of the Pacific Northwest, which is drenched by frequent rains and fed by rare sunshine.

These particular hills were part of Saturna Island, not far from the state of Washington. The long driveway led to a house nestled at the base of one of those hills. It was the home of John and Katherine McCormick and their two sons, Angus and Silas.

As the '68 Chevy pickup sped along the familiar route, John McCormick's blue eyes shifted from the driveway to his pretty wife. Her intelligent face, framed by brunette hair, looked serene.

"You think the boys are okay for a couple of hours?" he asked.

"They're fine," Katherine stated. "They can stay next door all day if we want."

McCormick wished he could feel as calm as Katherine about leaving Angus and Silas home alone while he and she made the trip into town. Angus was quite responsible and resourceful for thirteen, but seven-and-a-half-year-old Silas could be quite a handful. And, together with Angus' best friend, David . . .

"You never know what they're going to do," McCormick fretted.

"They're going to build a new laser weapon complex at the tree house," Katherine replied.

McCormick was confused. "*Whose* tree house?"

Katherine smiled. She loved her husband, but at times he could be amazingly oblivious.

"*Their* tree house," she answered before changing the subject. "You're getting the list of stuff for John Staviak in Winter Harbour?"

"Yes. There's propane for a couple of float camps, some machine parts," McCormick replied, hoping his voice sounded neutral.

"What's that, about five days you'll be gone?" Katherine persisted.

"Four or five," McCormick said vaguely.

"When we moved here, you told me that if I ever needed anything just to ask, right?" she said.

"Right," McCormick said.

"And I haven't asked for anything, right?" Katherine continued.

"Well, almost nothing," McCormick conceded. Actually, Katherine had been quite a sport about the change from living in the city to living in *the sticks*. Many spouses would have bolted during that first hard winter, not to mention the muddy season that followed.

McCormick's thoughts were interrupted by Katherine's indignant cry, "*What?*"

"Okay, nothing," McCormick agreed. "You've asked for nothing."

Katherine settled back more comfortably against the worn seat cushion. Victory was at hand. "You have to fix the dryer. I can't take one more day."

McCormick sighed guiltily. Katherine had been complaining about the dryer for quite a while now, but he simply hadn't been in the mood to fix it. That, and he wasn't exactly sure he *could*, which was something he didn't want to admit. "Okay," he said, feeling the silence grow tense. "Not another day."

Katherine smiled. "You're a good man, McCormick," she declared.

Another man might have objected to his wife calling him by his last name, but John preferred *McCormick* to *darling*.

Back at the McCormick house, Angus felt like Tarzan as he ran through the woods with David and Silas. His handsome face was smeared with war paint, which was really mud. His dark eyes were quick and alert, scanning the woods for game. His body was protected by "armor" made of cardboard and bark. And he carried a spear, which was actually a stick.

Angus' best friend, David, was outfitted the same way. But his brother, Silas, wore one of his homemade super-

9

hero suits. No one ever knew who Silas was going to be until he appeared at the breakfast table caped, helmeted, and masked.

Sometimes Silas announced his identity with a dramatic flourish and a loud fanfare of imaginary trumpets. On other mornings, Angus had to guess who was crunching the cereal beside him — Spider-Man, Elektro Boy, or the Masked Avenger?

At least there weren't enough people on Saturna Island for Silas' habit to be embarrassing. Every small community had to have its eccentrics.

Angus' thoughts were interrupted by leaves rustling in the nearby underbrush. Angus saw a fleeting glimpse of brown fur. "Rabbit!" he cried.

At the sound of the boy's voice, the hare sprang from cover and darted between the dense trees. Powerful hind legs pushed into the soft dirt and rose up again instantly as the animal streaked first in one direction, then another. One leap carried it over a rock, the next over a log.

The hare zigzagged wildly from cover to cover. He doubled back on his own tracks, but couldn't shake the largest of his three pursuers. The two-legged creature was surprisingly fast!

Angus had never felt quite so much the hunter before. It was as if the whole world had narrowed down to him and the rabbit. His feet knew what to do. They leaped over logs and fallen branches. They carried him closer and closer to the fleeing animal.

Angus burst out of the woods and found himself on the edge of a small cliff. The sea shimmered like a blue jewel below the rocks.

Chest heaving as he gasped for breath, Angus was eye to eye with his terrified prey. The hare's tiny chest heaved too. No longer having to glimpse through leaves, Angus could clearly see the animal for the first time. It was not a soft-furred rabbit at all, but a tough old hare with a scraggly coat.

The long ears trembled, but the hare gazed at Angus with a kind of resigned courage. Angus stared into the bright brown eyes. His fingers fumbled on the ground for a stone to arm his homemade slingshot.

Even as he looked at the hare, Angus felt someone was watching him from the woods. But it couldn't be David or Silas, or he would have heard them.

Angus ignored the creepy sensation and fitted a stone into the sling. He drew back the sling, taking careful aim.

Angus pictured the stone flying through the air and striking the velvety head. He pictured the hare falling. And he waited for his hands to accomplish the task, but they did not move except to lower the slingshot.

Angus heard David and Silas crashing through the trees behind him. Silas shouted, "Angus, did you get it?"

Angus tossed a stick at the old hare to send him on his way. "Get out of here. Get out," he muttered.

The hare blinked, then leaped into the green arms of the forest, just as the other two-legged creatures reached the cliff.

"Did you get it?" Silas repeated, panting. He adjusted the cape, which had shifted off one shoulder and now fluttered in the salty ocean breeze.

"Where is it? Where did it go?" David demanded eagerly.

11

"He got away," Angus said sheepishly.

"Where?" asked David as he surveyed the cliff.

"How did it get away?" Silas asked.

Angus felt funny about lying. He didn't even know why he'd let the hare go, and he certainly didn't feel up to explaining himself to David and Silas. "I'll just get him next time," Angus said.

"Yeah, you'll get him next time," Silas agreed.

Angus fired his slingshot toward the horizon and watched the rock drop with a satisfying SPLASH into the shining waves.

"Killer chase, though," David said.

"The best," Silas agreed. "Never going to see that rabbit again, no way."

"It was a hare, not a rabbit," Angus said.

"Never see that hare again," Silas corrected himself.

But Angus wasn't listening. Once again, he felt quite certain that someone was watching him from the woods.

Later that afternoon, the Chevy pickup chugged up Main Street to the town's best (and only) hardware store. Even after all this time, McCormick was still amazed that he could always find a parking spot on Main Street. In the city a good parking spot was more precious than a taxi in the rain. Everything was different here — and John McCormick liked it that way.

McCormick's strong arms were loaded with supplies: two top-quality life preservers, several boxes of brass screws, two cans of the finest marine enamel paint, brushes, and more. Katherine rounded the corner and met him halfway down the nearly deserted aisle.

"This paint wasn't on the list, McCormick," she chided.

McCormick unloaded several items into her care. "Angus is paying for his own boat stuff, Kath. He's just having a little trouble getting the cash," McCormick explained.

Katherine sighed. She did not approve of lapses in discipline. The whole point of discipline was to be consistent. Didn't McCormick understand that?

"The deal was, Angus has to finish his own boat with his own money, right?" said Katherine.

"He'll pay me back." McCormick moved down the aisle, toward the counter.

Katherine shook her head. "You know he's going to end up spending it on something else. I don't know why you do this."

"It'll be okay," McCormick said, putting the things down on the counter. He was glad to see the manager, Ron Willick, who was waiting to ring up the sale. Ron's presence meant end-of-discussion.

"How's it going today, guys?" Willick asked.

"Perfect, Ron," McCormick and Katherine answered at the same time.

Katherine smiled and emptied the contents of her arms on the scratched counter. She knew Willick would want to chat, and she wasn't in the mood. They'd already been to several stores and in each there had been the necessary small-town chat. And she was too annoyed about the paint to be in the mood for more.

"See you, Ron. I'll be in the truck, McCormick," Katherine said coolly.

"Be right there," McCormick called after her, but Katherine was already gone.

13

CHAPTER

2

hile Katherine brooded over the marine-paint purchase, three "hunters" ran across the fields in front of the McCormick home. Silas spread his cape to the wind and pumped his shorter legs to keep up with his brother and David.

Before long, another pair of feet pounded the green-carpeted earth. They belonged to Sara, a girl who lived nearby. Like Angus, Sara was thirteen. Though she shared all his boyish interests, Sara was also interested in *boys* — specifically in Angus.

The boys did not slow their pace. But Sara easily kept up with them. "Where are you going?" she asked.

"To work on the boat," Angus replied.

Soon, the runners reached a huge old barn that stood at the edge of the woods. When Angus threw open the door, shafts of sunlight flooded the dim interior and fell on his pride and joy.

Twelve feet long of lovingly crafted wood, the boat was four feet wide and one-and-a-half feet deep. Angus couldn't count the times he'd pounded his thumb with the hammer, suffered painful splinters, or just plain exhausted himself with work. But he'd never doubted for a moment that the boat was worth every hard-earned penny and drop of sweat.

Angus took a moment to admire his handiwork. Dad had helped, of course. But the boat belonged to Angus — every plank. And soon it would be ready for the sea.

The boat already had two sets of oars. The mast was built, but not yet fitted in place. As soon as it got an outboard motor, some finishing touches, and a few coats of paint, it would be ready for anything!

Angus immediately set to work planing a piece of wood. He held the tool securely in both hands and stroked it firmly but smoothly along the surface of the board, just the way Dad had showed him.

David walked around the carefully constructed wooden scaffolding holding the boat off the barn floor. Even though Angus was his best friend, David couldn't help feeling a bit jealous — not only of the wonderful boat, but of all the time Angus gave to it.

"Great boat," David said. "When are you going to finish it?"

"We'll have to set the tiller and put the hardware on it," Angus replied, not looking up from his work. The tiller would steer the finished boat. Dad said the plain bar tiller would be better than a wheel for moving the rudder for this size boat.

"After that, you have to paint it," Silas added.

15

"*Then* are you going to take it out?" David demanded.

"Next week, if we finish," Angus replied. "I need to get more money from someplace."

Sara surveyed the boat carefully. "I could give you some money," she offered.

Angus felt a bit embarrassed. So he smoothed one of the gunwales edging the boat's top side and said, "I think I'll get enough."

"You could probably go to South America in this thing," Silas suggested.

"Who'd want to?" David wondered. "There's nothing left there."

"Sure there is," Silas said.

"What?" David challenged.

"The Amazon, countless species of wildlife . . ." Silas began.

"Okay, so one thing," David conceded.

While Silas and David argued, Sara picked up a screwdriver and idly tightened a screw. Angus felt the hairs on his neck rise. His eyes followed Sara's every movement. It made him nervous when anyone else but Dad touched the boat.

"I'm taking it to Winter Harbour," Angus told Sara proudly.

"By yourself?" she asked.

"Next week, when my Dad goes," Angus explained.

Sara put down the screwdriver and picked up a baseball. She watched specks of dust swirl through the sunlight as she tossed the ball up into the rafters.

Silas wandered closer to join in the conversation. He kicked his toe through the sawdust on the floor.

"I'm too small to go," he said, hoping Angus would contradict him.

"How long are you going to be away?" Sara asked.

Angus watched her throw the ball up once more and catch it expertly. Sara really was all right for a girl. "Five days, about. Dad said I could miss school for a day or two."

Sara smiled. "That's great." She would miss Angus, but she was happy for him.

Angus never liked waking up early to deliver newspapers. But once he was on his trusty mountain bike, he always felt good. David pedaled alongside. Behind them, Silas' superhero cape flapped in the breeze as the boys rode a wooded path. Through the trees, Angus spotted the bright shimmer of morning sunlight on the water of Horton Bay.

When the boys stopped, they saw Mr. McCormick's boat, the *Cormorant,* tied to the dock. It was a sixty-foot-long ocean workboat, all business. But to Angus, it was also beautiful.

The boys jumped off their bikes and ran the length of the creaking, wooden dock. Angus took the lead, followed by David, then Silas a fair ways behind.

"You guys owe me if I do it," Angus called into the wind.

"There's no way," Silas panted. "It's too cold."

Angus knew it was cold. But he also knew he could take it. As his feet left the dock, he knew he'd *have* to take it! For a moment, Angus lingered in the cool, ocean breeze. Then came the SPLASH, quickly followed by another splash, as David jumped in too.

17

Silas stood at the end of the dock and watched for bubbles to rise to the surface.

"Those guys are nuts," he muttered.

When no bubbles appeared, Silas walked to the other side of the dock and stared into the deep green water. Angus' dark head popped up first, then David's.

"There's something under the wrecked dock," Angus reported. He scrambled back onto the dock, wet clothes flattened against his taut muscles.

David scrambled up beside him, teeth chattering. "It's too cold."

"I'm going to get it." Angus' full lips were set in a determined grin.

Silas knew that expression. Angus could do anything he set his mind to, but Silas didn't always understand why Angus set his mind to one thing and not to another. "What is it, you guys?"

Angus didn't answer, he just dived in. Despite his chattering teeth, David dived in after. Silas watched their limbs move through the green depths as the older boys swam deeper. He realized they were swimming toward the remains of an old, ruined dock.

Through a forest of broken, rotted beams, Angus spotted part of a sunken boat. To him, it was as sad as a skeleton, the wooden frame half-buried in sand and stones.

Angus saw sunlight wink off something almost completely hidden in silt and barnacles. He pulled himself along the edge of the wreckage to grab the object. David's hands joined in the tugging. Mud rose in a soft cloud as the object came loose.

From the dock, Silas could see nothing. He scratched

his helmet thoughtfully. The suspense was worse than the freezing water, so in he jumped! As the two older boys made off with their treasure, Silas swam deeper, his cape flowing out behind him.

Maybe I'm Marine Boy today, he thought. Silas reached the old submerged dock in time to see Angus' and David's feet kicking up to the surface.

David helped Angus haul their booty onto the dock. They brushed off the top layer of seaweed and saw a glass bubble set in a round, wooden frame. To David, it looked like one of those old-fashioned clocks some people have on their fireplace mantles — the kind of thing most grown-ups had a heart attack if you touched. But the face under the dirty glass didn't look like any clock face David had ever seen.

"What is it?" he asked.

"A marine compass. An old one," Angus replied. Suddenly, his stomach dropped to his toes. There was the feeling again, of eyes watching him, the same feeling he'd had when he'd let the hare go. But worse than that, where was Silas?

Silas thrashed frantically. He hadn't seen the beam fall, but had only felt his progress suddenly halted. Now his cape was stuck under the heavy pole. Stale air longed to escape his tight chest, but Silas held his breath. His eyes popped in panic as he desperately struggled to remove his costume.

Angus' heart beat frantically against his soggy T-shirt. Silas wouldn't just leave, but he might have tried to follow them. After all, that's what little brothers do.

David felt his friend's fear. He scanned the empty dock.

19

There were the three mountain bikes, just where the boys had left them. Then his eyes turned to the rippling water.

"He's not here," David said. Just then Silas' helmet bobbed to the surface. Without needing to speak or even decide, both boys dived into the sea. Someone else dived in too.

Angus swam faster than he knew he could and soon reached his brother. Bracing himself against a beam, Angus tried to pull Silas free. Angus knew Silas couldn't hold his breath much longer.

Angus was suddenly aware of someone else moving through the murky water. Yellowish fur tinted green by the sea covered four busily paddling legs.

It's a dog, Angus realized, just as the creature's pointed muzzle reached Silas.

Sharp teeth ripped at the flowing cape and yanked it free of the beam. Silas shot toward the surface like a missile. Angus and David swam up to each grab one of his hands.

Silas coughed and sputtered as Angus and David held his face above the rippling water. They dragged him onto the dock as the yellow dog pulled himself out of the water. Droplets rained from the dog's thick tawny coat as he shook himself dry. A torn fragment of Silas' cape still hung from the dog's powerful jaws.

The dog's intelligent brown eyes watched as Angus and David tried to pump the water out of Silas. Salt water splattered the dock as Silas coughed and coughed again. Angus hugged his brother close to him. His head swam with a dizzying mixture of fear and relief.

David stood nearby, not knowing what to do. A boy

couldn't have any fun if he didn't take any chances. But it sure was scary to come that close to . . . It was too scary to even *think* about how close Silas had come.

"Don't do that again, okay! I'll get killed if I don't look after you," Angus scolded.

"I was looking for you guys," Silas explained. "I thought you froze."

Angus turned from his brother's small, freckled face to watch the yellow dog, who was further down the dock ripping Silas' cape to shreds. The dog dropped the cape and stared at Angus. Angus stared back. He knew that stare. It was the same stare he'd felt hunting the other day. The dog had been following them — but why?

The dog returned Angus' gaze and barked once.

"He tried to kill Silas," David accused.

"He tried to pull him out," Angus corrected. "He won't hurt us."

"Where'd he come from then?" David challenged. If anyone was going to get blamed for Silas almost drowning, he wanted it to be the dog.

Angus regarded the dog. He was a yellow Labrador retriever. The wet fur topping his muscular body was a deep yellow. The fur on his chest and underside was the soft white of vanilla pudding. Velvety ears hung on either side of his large head. A large, black nose tipped the wide muzzle. He was a beautiful dog. Angus was glad to see that no collar circled the strong neck.

"He's nobody's dog," Angus declared.

"Maybe he fell out of the sky from heaven," Silas proposed. After all, the dog had saved his life, like Superman suddenly appearing to catch Lois Lane as she fell from a building. And Superman had sort of come from heaven.

Angus took a tentative step toward the dog. Then his ears were filled with a familiar roar.

The dog's eyes grew wide with fear. All four legs left the ground at once as he raced up the dock, away from the terrifying noise. He looked back once at Angus, before disappearing into the woods.

"It's the plane," Angus said. "We've got to get the papers."

The seaplane's white pontoons touched the rippling waters. Jeremy Cooper, the pilot, hurried out of the cockpit to tie up his craft, then help a lone passenger onto the dock. He went back to the plane for the heavy bundles of newspapers.

"How many customers have you got now?" Cooper asked, as he tossed down the first bundle.

"Seventy-eight," Angus said. "And sixteen more on Sundays."

Cooper looked up from the papers to the wet, mud-streaked boys. "What happened to you guys?"

"Nothing," they said together.

Cooper grinned. He remembered when he was a boy and got into lots of "nothing" himself. He untied the plane and pushed off from the dock. "See you tomorrow," he called to the boys, adding to Silas, "So long, Spider-Man!"

Cooper started the seaplane, but over the engine he could still hear Silas' reply. "Electric Shock Man!"

Cooper yelled over the din, "Electric Shock Man!"

The seaplane taxied away from the dock, then lifted into the sky like a noisy white bird.

CHAPTER

3

hat evening in the barn, Angus and Silas scraped layer after layer of mud off the old compass. Sara watched the brothers working, now and then handing them a clean rag. Only a few scratches marred the glass.

"What does it do?" Silas asked.

"Tells you where you are," Angus explained. "If you have one of these, you can't get lost." He had long since learned to give simple answers to Silas' questions — or he'd end up answering more questions all night.

Silas' blond head nodded solemnly. "I get it," he said with more certainty than he felt. "So they know where to find you."

"Kind of like that," Angus replied. "It keeps you on a straight line."

"If you know how to read it," added Sara.

"It's a good one," Angus declared. "Might be worth a

couple of dollars."

Sara's eyes widened with surprise. It was such a lovely old compass, a romantic relic of seafaring days gone by. How could Angus even think of selling it?

John McCormick was thinking of selling his truck. He'd been thinking of selling it for years, but could never quite bring himself to do it. Now he was teaching his young son to drive that truck, and somehow that felt right, like passing down a family tradition. Of course, it would feel better if Angus knew what he was doing.

The old Chevy bounced across the fields that stretched in front of the McCormick house. The day's last sunlight tinted everything a mellow gold, but McCormick was blind to its beauty. He was too busy hanging on for dear life!

"Do I shift yet?" Angus asked. His voice shook with the bouncing truck.

"Sure, okay, into second," McCormick agreed, trying to sound calmer than he felt. "Don't give it quite so much gas. Ease off the gas."

Angus hit the gas and the clutch at the same time. The truck bucked like a bronco. McCormick winced at the grind of protesting gears as the Chevy shifted into second gear.

"The clutch! The clutch!" McCormick cried.

"Yeah, okay, I'm sorry," Angus said hastily lifting his foot from the gas. Driving was more confusing than it looked, but he didn't want Dad to give up on him. "I know I shouldn't have hit the gas and the clutch and shifted."

The truck turned off the rutted farm road and onto the McCormick's long driveway. Angus eased back onto the

24

gas gently. The truck sped up. "We're okay now."

McCormick tried to smile as he watched his son wrestle the Chevy's large steering wheel. There was just time to think *maybe the boy's too young* before the truck plowed into the neat pile of firewood that had taken McCormick three hours to stack. With loud THUNKs, logs landed everywhere. The truck finally stopped.

"Darn!" said Angus.

He climbed out of the truck, quickly followed by his father. Angus started clearing logs away from in front of the bumper. "It just fell over, just like that," Angus said.

He risked a quick glance at his father's face.

"Too bad it was so neatly stacked," McCormick said dryly. He wasn't old enough to forget his own father teaching him how to drive. Now that he was on the other end of the lessons, McCormick wondered how his old man had ever survived.

Angus nodded, feeling relieved. Then they both saw the shattered glass.

"Headlight's busted," McCormick stated. He didn't relish telling Katherine about that.

Angus swallowed hard. Headlights cost money. He stamped his foot on the ground, wishing he'd stamped on the brake. But it was too late.

Later, when the sun was just a memory in the glowing sky, Angus swung his father's ax onto the edge of a fat log. THUNK! The wood made a satisfying sound as it split neatly down the middle.

Angus bent to set one of the halves on its edge, then swung the ax again. THUNK! He tossed the slender pieces

25

of wood onto a large pile of kindling. Angus didn't mind splitting wood, but he couldn't help thinking that this evening the work felt like penance for the broken headlight. Oh well. At least Dad hadn't said he'd never take Angus driving again. Mom had been mad, but not that mad.

Angus wiped sweat off his brow. The muscles of his back clenched as he picked up a pile of kindling to bring inside for the woodstove.

Crickets hummed in the twilight. Frogs peeped and croaked to each other from the trees. At this hour the pines looked like black arrows aimed at the sky. The house was just a darker shape against a dark hill.

Angus stopped walking when he saw another shape standing at the bend in the driveway. Before he recognized the contour as a dog, Angus felt the yellow dog's presence, its stare.

Angus' arms fell limply to his sides, and the wood dropped to the ground. He stared back at the shape, hoping he could walk closer without scaring the dog away.

Angus approached, and the dog stayed where he was. Angus whistled, and the dog barked once, quietly. Angus held the dog's steady stare as he crept closer.

"Good dog," he said gently. "Where did you come from?"

The dog didn't move and never stopped staring. Angus stopped at a respectful distance and held out his hand. He knew enough about animals to know that it was polite to let them sniff you first.

Angus knelt down and kept his hand stretched out toward the black-tipped muzzle. "Come on, boy. Come on."

The dog whined softly and held his ground as Angus

reached out for him. Soft fur, wet nose, warm breath —
Angus felt a shock of pleasure. He had touched the yellow
dog!

McCormick's callused hands rubbed the dog's sturdy
back. Through the thick yellow fur he felt the dog's
backbone. "He's a little thin and his coat's kind of rough,
isn't it?" he asked.

The entire McCormick clan was gathered outside the
farmhouse's front door to examine Angus' new friend.
Katherine would not pet the stranger. The last thing she
wanted was another mouth to feed and clean up after.

"I'm sure it belongs to someone," she said.

"No, he doesn't," Silas said.

Angus gave his brother a quick nudge with his elbow.
Silas was glad it was too dark for his mother to see him
blush. They hadn't told her about what had happened at
the dock. If they had, the boys would be grounded for life.

"I mean, I don't think so. He doesn't have a collar or
nothing," Silas said hastily.

"Doesn't have a collar or *anything*," Katherine corrected.

"He hasn't got a home," Angus said. He was as sure of
that as if the dog had told him.

"He could be lost," Silas suggested.

"Dogs don't get lost," Angus said. His dark eyes flashed
a warning to Silas. The less his little brother said, the
better.

Silas nodded. "Right."

McCormick sighed. He loved dogs, but he knew how
Katherine felt on the subject of pets. "Let's call the animal
shelter and ask them . . ."

Angus looked at his father. Despite the dim light, McCormick could clearly read the anguish in his son's eyes. "They'll put him to sleep," Angus said.

". . . and ask them if someone has reported a missing dog," McCormick finished his sentence. "He probably belongs to some summer people." Many people came up to Saturna Island for the cool summers. Few stayed to weather the winters, which was why McCormick liked the island so much.

Angus' face lit up like a beacon. "If nobody claims him, can we keep him?"

Katherine looked at her husband and sighed. That was it. What could they say? "We'll put an ad in the paper and phone around tomorrow," she said.

Angus' heart swelled with hope and joy. "Okay, so we'll keep him until someone calls?" He held his breath waiting for his mother's answer.

"We'll give it a couple of days."

McCormick's hand strayed to the dog's bony back. "We'll see what happens," he agreed.

Angus grinned. He knelt down to be closer to the dog. "Are you hungry, dog?"

Katherine looked to her husband nervously. "We don't want to feed it, do we? It'll hang around forever."

Four pairs of eyes regarded her expectantly. Three mouths spoke at once, "He's really hungry. We have to feed him something!"

"All right," said Katherine. "But it stays outside." She felt like a general who had already lost the war, but was still drawing boundaries across the battlefield.

"He will," Angus promised. And feeling as if he were

walking on clouds, he led the dog to the woodshed beside the chicken coop.

A few hours later, boy and dog were snuggled cozily on Angus' bed. The dog's snores played a gentle bass to the boy's slow, steady breathing.

The next afternoon, Angus and Silas rode their mountain bikes up a lonely hill overlooking a rundown farm. The yellow dog ran alongside them. Angus' empty newspaper sack flapped against his back. A single paper lay in the bottom of Silas' bag.

The boys stopped their bikes and contemplated the long ride to the farmhouse. The yellow dog stopped running. His panting tongue hung out.

Silas handed the last paper to his brother, along with the money they'd collected so far. Angus put the cash in his pocket and thought of the boat.

"Throw it on the porch and let's get out of here," Silas urged. The creepy farmhouse was almost as scary as its occupants.

Angus shook his head. "I've got to collect. The guy owes us for months, and I have to pay for the boat and the darn headlight too."

Silas swallowed hard. He didn't like admitting he was afraid. Superheroes weren't supposed to be afraid. "We could borrow some money."

Angus handed the yellow dog's rope leash to his brother. "Hang on to the dog."

His lips set in a determined grimace, Angus rode across an untended orchard toward the sagging farmhouse. The yellow dog tugged at the rope in Silas' hand. Since Angus had touched his nose in the driveway, boy and dog had hardly parted.

Angus dropped his bike in front of the farmhouse. Tense with dread, he listened intently as he scanned the weedy yard.

Suddenly the silence was broken by the clatter of toenails on boards and deep savage barking. One-hundred-and-seventy pounds of canine fury burst from the farmhouse basement and leaped at Angus.

The boy jumped aside, just beyond reach of the Rottweiler's chain. Two rows of sharp teeth snapped together. A low terrible growl escalated into deafening barks.

Sweat prickled up Angus' back. He hated that dog; and worse than that, Angus feared it. But he would not back down.

Silas' feet left the ground before he realized what was happening. Enraged by the Rottweiler's bark, the yellow dog had taken off like a rocket. Still holding the other end of the dog's leash, Silas was pulled off his bike and through the muddy weeds. He gained his feet for a few steps, then fell again, only to be dragged by the unstoppable yellow dog.

"AnnGGggGGuuuSsss!" Silas' voice bounced along with his body.

At that moment, Angus was having his own problems. The furious Rottweiler tugged at his chain. Black muscles bulged beneath the short fur. The metal links looked thin and frail, ready to break at any second.

Angus hopped from one foot to the other. "Paper! Collecting! PAPER!" he shouted.

The only answer was more barking. Angus glanced at the feeble chain and chucked the newspaper onto the porch. It hit the front door right in the center, but bounced back down to the foot of the rotting stairs. The Rottweiler trotted over to the paper and ripped it to shreds.

Angus shouted, "Hey, Mr. Bennett!"

The Rottweiler lunged at the boy, snapping his chain taut once more — and this time very nearly catching Angus in his gaping jaws.

Angus was pedaling almost before he had his bike upright again. He found Silas struggling to tie the yellow dog's rope around a tree. The dog took off at the sight of Angus, dragging Silas after him once more.

"Quit playing with the dog!" Angus chided. "Let's get out of here!" He was angry at Mr. Bennett for cheating them out of the money, angry at the Rottweiler for being such a beast, and angry at Silas for kidding around. But by the time Angus had untangled the muddy mess of rope, dog, and little brother, he was laughing. Things were certainly more fun with the yellow dog!

CHAPTER

4

 hat night, the yellow dog watched the porch swing rock slowly back and forth, back and forth. The man and woman held each other close and kissed.

"They're asleep," Katherine said.

"Yeah, they are," McCormick agreed.

Katherine leaned toward her husband again, lips puckered. But her cheek was tickled by soft whiskers. Warm breath rose from a panting pink tongue that definitely did not belong to McCormick. Katherine looked into the eager brown eyes. "They forgot to feed the dog," she concluded.

The yellow dog's tail wagged happily. The woman understood!

Soon, kibble clattered into the plastic mixing bowl the McCormicks were using as the dog's temporary dish. The yellow dog gobbled happily. Humans could be trained. All a dog needed was patience!

The next morning, Katherine was cleaning up after breakfast when she felt that stare boring into her back. She turned and saw the yellow dog watching her scrape leftover bacon and egg off the plates piled on the counter.

"Bet you don't even know how to sit," she said.

The yellow dog promptly settled his haunches on the floor. Katherine's eyes widened in surprise. Then she decided it was just a coincidence. The dog had been meaning to sit down anyway.

"Lie down," she commanded, sure he wouldn't.

The yellow dog lay down on the floor.

Katherine tried to remember something else people told their dogs to do. "Um . . . heel?" she tried.

The yellow dog approached her, circled behind, and then settled himself at her left side like a well-trained soldier standing at attention before the next command. Katherine's hand went up to her mouth.

Heel meant he would follow her wherever she went and stop when she did, right? Katherine took a few steps away from the dog. He followed — at her heels! And when she stopped, the dog stopped and sat once more. It was like having a furry shadow.

"Okay, okay, stop," Katherine said. Then she held out the plate of scraps. "Here . . ." she began. But the dog had already licked the plate clean.

The yellow dog might have been trained, but he certainly wasn't a model student from an obedience school. One afternoon, Angus, Silas, David, and Sara were playing baseball near the McCormick's farmhouse.

David pitched a fast ball to Angus, who swung at air. The ball bounced across the grass and the yellow dog pounced on it. He shook the ball between his jaws and growled.

Silas was the catcher, so he wrestled the dog for the ball. "Ahhhgh! It's got spit all over it."

Angus was impatient. Not only did he want to play baseball, he didn't like anyone criticizing the yellow dog — no matter how annoying the dog could be!

"Just throw it, okay!" Angus yelled.

So Silas threw the ball to David. And David pitched one Angus could hit and . . . The ball sailed like a comet, high over the lawn. It whacked into the clean sheets hanging on the clothesline.

The yellow dog leaped for the ball. Four ferocious paws tore at the clean laundry, dragging it down into the mud! The clothesline fell to the muddy ground. Then the dog streaked off into the trees in a blur of yellow.

Sometimes Angus felt as if the dog were giving his mother reasons for not letting the family keep him. He just wouldn't behave!

One afternoon, Angus saw the yellow dog running away from the chicken coop. Actually, what he saw was a flash of yellow fur and white feathers as the dog charged the chickens. The yellow dog chased several frantic squawking birds through thick underbrush. Their feeble flapping wings carried them briefly above the ferns, only to land on their yellow feet again.

Angus chased the dog. But he didn't catch him until two chickens were dead in a heap of feathers. Angus grabbed the rope collar circling the dog's neck.

"Bad dog!" he shouted. Messing up laundry was bad enough, but if the dog was a chicken killer, no way would Angus' parents keep him.

Angus scooped up a terrified chicken. The bird was too exhausted to resist. Angus felt its heart beating wildly against his hands.

Silas arrived, panting. His blue eyes were round with worry. "There were three, Angus."

Angus nodded impatiently. He also had counted three chickens in the chase.

"There's only one now," Silas reported miserably.

Angus was all too aware of that fact.

"He ate them. Dad's going to kill us!" Silas cried.

"It was the raccoon!" Angus said. That had to be it. The yellow dog wasn't a chicken killer. It only looked that way. He must have been chasing a raccoon away from the coop. The McCormicks had trouble with raccoons before.

Silas shook his head. "No. It was him."

Angus sighed. "Don't you get it? It wasn't the dog, okay! I'm going to have to pay for these two dead chickens now."

Silas nodded.

"Come on, we've got to get rid of this mess before Dad sees it," Angus declared.

After dinner, the elder McCormicks had a serious talk with Angus at the kitchen table. The yellow dog sat with Angus, bright eyes darting to whoever was speaking.

John ran a hand through his pale hair. "I don't care how they got out. You were supposed to keep the gate closed so nothing would get them."

"It wasn't the dog," Angus argued.

"I know it wasn't the dog. That isn't the point," McCormick said. Actually, McCormick wasn't sure about Angus' story, but he couldn't face the idea of trying to part boy and dog now. They had already grown so close. He could feel his son's dark eyes begging.

"We can't have a dog," Katherine stated.

"I'll take care of him," Angus promised.

Katherine sighed. "It's more than that, Angus. You have to clean up after it, buy food for it. If we go somewhere, who's going to take care of it?"

"We're already somewhere, not in the city anymore," Angus said. Why would they move to a wonderful place like Saturna Island and then go somewhere else on vacation?

"What if it gets sick?" Katherine demanded.

Angus opened the yellow dog's mouth. "He won't get sick, look at his teeth."

There was a long uncomfortable silence.

"It's already two chickens and one headlight, as well as the boat paint," McCormick said at last. "That's about one hundred and thirty dollars. Do you know how much a dog is going to be?"

An even longer silence followed, during which Angus made an agonizing decision. "I'll keep him, and we can take the paint back, if that's okay."

His parents stared at each other. Angus had chosen the dog over his precious boat. This was love — and how could they argue with that?

"He's your dog then, Angus," Katherine concluded. "He's your responsibility."

Angus buried his face in the dog's furry neck to hide

his grateful tears.

On the McCormick's next trip to town, Angus headed straight for the hardware store. He waited at the counter, which was heaped with dog supplies, including bright red plastic dishes and a fifty-pound sack of kibble.

Angus drummed his fingers impatiently while Ron Willick finished working the metal stamp machine. Finally, Ron held out the red collar, along with a license tag and a brass disc punched with the name Angus had chosen.

"Here's his collar and license," Ron said. "And the name tag. Good name."

Angus stared at the tag resting in his palm. The brass disc spelled out YELLOW DOG. Somehow every other name had seemed phony or just hadn't suited the dog at all.

"Thanks," Angus replied. Then he remembered what he'd been planning to ask. "That bag of dog food has the special-offer whistle in it, right?"

Willick examined the large paper sack. Bold type proclaimed the special offer. "That's what it says here."

Angus smiled. Ron rang up the sale. When the total appeared, Angus' eyes bulged in surprise. "$52.85?"

Ron didn't answer. The four green numbers spoke for him. Angus shoved several crumpled bills across the counter. He didn't want to think of how many papers he had to deliver to earn that much money. Instead, he thought of Yellow Dog.

"Sure you can handle all this stuff?" Ron asked.

Angus nodded. "Yeah, sure, Mr. Willick."

"See you," Willick called after him. But the boy had nearly disappeared behind the giant bag of kibble as he staggered through the door.

That evening outside the farmhouse, Angus eagerly ripped into the bag and poured a pile of kibble into Yellow Dog's shiny new food dish. A small silver-colored plastic whistle fell into the red dish too.

Angus reached past Yellow Dog's greedy muzzle to pick up the whistle. While the dog chomped, Angus brought the whistle to his lips and blew. A beautiful clear note echoed through the green hills.

Yellow Dog looked up from his dish and woofed.

Angus stared at the whistle. He'd expected something junky, like the toys you find in cereal boxes. But this whistle was great! He blew it again, and the same pure tone rang through the valley.

Yellow Dog woofed. He liked the whistle too.

Angus untied the dirty rope collar circling the dog's neck. He put on the new collar with its shiny tags.

"Good dog," said Angus.

The next day, McCormick and his friend, John Gale, were in the barn fixing the clothes dryer. The battered old machine looked as if it were ready for that great laundromat in the sky, but McCormick was determined to save it. Saving was Gale's business. His muscular torso was encased in a blue Search and Rescue sweatshirt.

McCormick loosened the last screw and pulled out the dryer's rusty thermostat. He walked across the barn to the area delegated to spare parts. "It's the thermostat," he said.

Gale nodded. "Always is."

"At least we can do it ourselves, instead of waiting weeks for some overpaid, underqualified guy in a jump suit to do it," McCormick said. Actually, he wouldn't have minded turning the task over to someone else, but finding a repairman on Saturna Island was not at all like in the city, where the fat phone book listed dozens of companies. The Saturna Island phone book was more like a brochure than a book.

As if reading McCormick's mind, Gale replied, "One of the inconveniences of living in the wild, McCormick — no company repairmen."

McCormick's blue eyes grew distant with memories. "Small price to pay for not being caged in an office ten hours a day."

Gale nodded. "Good point."

Gale was sick of dryers, which were always breaking. So he wandered across the barn where Angus was working on the boat. The boy was fitting a seat in place. Gale regarded the lovingly built craft. "What is that, oak or fir?"

Angus smiled. When it came to the boat, he was as bad as a boastful grandma. He could talk about the boat all day. "Fir," he replied. "Twelve feet, eight inches. Beam is four feet, ten and one half inches. Brass fittings. We're going to build the mast and sail next year."

Gale admired the neat job. "This'll hold up in rough water."

Angus nodded happily. "We're going to put in a place under the seat to stash stuff, like for camping."

Gale looked at the boat more closely. The more he looked, the more he found to admire. It was a perfect little craft. "That's terrific."

Angus smiled. That's exactly what he thought.

That night in a nearby clearing, Angus, Silas, and David pitched a tent. As the boys worked, Yellow Dog watched, giving an occasional *woof* of encouragement.

While David dug a trench around the tent, Silas gathered stones. Angus watched his father stack the stones in a circle. Dad wasn't going to sleep out with the boys, but he had come along to help them set up.

McCormick wanted to teach his sons as much as he could about the woods. "Build a chimney so air feeds the fire from underneath."

McCormick arranged a few stones and Angus added more. "The rocks work like a windbreak and reflect heat," Angus recalled from Dad's last fire lesson.

McCormick smiled. "Right."

McCormick looked from the fire to the large cardboard box beside the tent. So much for traveling light. "Got enough food for the night?" he asked sarcastically.

"We got a whole box, Dad," Silas said proudly.

McCormick chuckled to himself. Sarcasm was usually lost on Silas. "Gather up a bunch of insects," he told the boys. It was time they learned that food didn't have to come from the store.

Silas looked confused. Why on earth would Dad want them to gather insects? Silas had tried to collect bugs, but Dad always told him to set them free.

McCormick said, "Moths, dragonflies, bees, wood bugs, snails, worms. All good."

Suddenly Silas understood his father's meaning. Good

40

for food! "That would taste terrible!"

McCormick shook his head. "Ants taste terrible, because there's too much acid in them. The rest are full of protein."

Angus could see where his father was going. You couldn't always count on having enough food with you on a camping trip. But bugs were everywhere. "You can mix them with berries or something, anyhow," his father suggested.

McCormick lifted a dead dragonfly from a nearby rock. "And they stop moving around if you crush them first."

Silas' freckled face contorted with disgust. David stuck his finger in his mouth and muttered, "Gag me!" but not loud enough for Mr. McCormick to hear.

Angus, on the other hand, looked thoughtfully at the dragonfly's plump body. Bugs were good protein. That was something to remember.

McCormick rose and brushed the dirt off his knees. "See you guys in the morning. Angus is in charge of the fire."

Angus felt proud of being in charge. "See you, Dad."

"See you, Mr. McCormick," David said.

Silas waved to his father. "Later, dude."

CHAPTER

5

 cCormick wasn't gone long before it started raining. Soon there was no fire left for Angus to douse. The boys huddled inside their tent with Yellow Dog, who happily gnawed a bone.

David tried to fix the wire antenna along the ridge-pole of the tent. If they couldn't roast marshmallows, at least they could listen to shortwave radio. Silas pressed buttons, but couldn't get anything more than static.

Droplets of rain splashed on the sleeping bags, down the tent seams, and everywhere else the boys looked. Angus moved his bag away from one leak and into another. Thunder boomed. Lightning flashed outside the soggy canvas walls. A garble of Russian voices suddenly blurted from the radio.

"Pull the antenna down," Angus said. "There's too much lightning."

"Maybe we'll get zapped." Silas thought getting struck

by lightning would be a good way to gain super powers.

Angus knew getting hit by lightning would be a good way to become a human French fry. "Pull it down, you guys!" he shrieked.

But when David and Silas just stared at him, Angus yanked down the antenna himself.

"Hey don't!" Silas protested.

Yellow Dog watched the argument between the brothers. He hoped they would wrestle so he could join in.

The light was dazzling, even through the tent, when a bolt of lightning split a nearby tree. Sparks crackled around the tree and branches crashed to the ground.

"Let's get out of here!" Angus screamed over the noisy storm.

"Yeah, let's," Silas agreed.

Angus peeked out the tent flap at the pouring rain. He wrapped himself in his sleeping bag and threw Silas' bag over his shoulders.

David looked out at the raging storm and hesitated. Going out seemed almost worse than staying. But, he reminded himself, it wasn't that far to the McCormick house. "I don't want to get zapped," he said, wrapping his sleeping bag tightly around him and clutching his flashlight.

"Come on, you guys." Angus hoped he didn't sound as afraid as he felt. Rain sparkled in his flashlight's beam as the boys and Yellow Dog left the tent.

Suddenly the whole sky was bright with the biggest bolt of lightning Angus had ever seen. The trees looked like black skeletons against the black sky. Their wet bark glistened with a ghostly shine.

Angus looked away from the frightening scene. They were definitely right to be going home.

McCormick met the wet boys and dog on the farmhouse porch. So much for his romantic evening alone with Katherine.

Angus tried not to look frightened in front of his father. Shivering from the wet didn't help. Angus blinked as McCormick's huge flashlight illuminated his face.

"You know, the tent, it started leaking," Angus hastily explained. "It was sort of wet already, and then the lightning hit."

McCormick was glad the boys had come in. "Are you guys okay?"

"Yeah, we're fine," Angus declared.

McCormick ushered them inside. "Go on inside and get some dry clothes on."

At dawn, Angus and his father were already hard at work in the barn. They filled a sturdy wooden box with supplies. "Fishing line and hooks," McCormick said.

"Crackers, cook pot, tarp," Angus added.

"That's it. The camp kit," McCormick concluded. He closed the tightly fitted, rubber-sealed lid. Then he looked at his son. This was the right moment. McCormick produced a small old cardboard box.

"This is yours," he said. "It goes to the next boat's master."

Angus opened the box. Inside lay a very old Swiss army knife. Angus recognized the white cross on the red handle. The knife looked ancient, but it was wonderfully made and very well-cared for. "This was *your* father's?"

44

McCormick nodded. "Yes, it was."

Angus felt too excited to speak. Instead, he opened the knife to examine all seven blade attachments.

"It's fantastic," he said.

McCormick smiled. "You see, there's a fish knife as well as a small cutting blade, and an awl for working sailcloth." He remembered admiring that knife back when he was a boy, and the stern skipper who had wielded it so skillfully. McCormick remembered that much more clearly than the frail old man his father later became.

"How old is it?" Angus wondered.

"About sixty, sixty-five years old. Still perfect," McCormick answered proudly.

Angus echoed, "It's perfect."

Early morning light winked on the perfectly polished blade.

That afternoon, Yellow Dog watched as Angus and Silas finished painting the boat. The dog yawned sleepily. Sunshine poured in through the barn's big double-doors, lending a rich glow to the bright red paint. Splatters and splashes covered the barn floor — and Silas and Angus — but the boat looked wonderful.

Angus stood up and noticed for the first time that his shoulder was aching from moving the paintbrush up and down, up and down. Despite the pain, he smiled. The boat was done!

As soon as the paint was dry, McCormick brought Angus' boat to the bay. He watched from the dock as Angus pulled the oars. Angus' face showed signs of strain

45

as he rocked back and forth with the hard work of rowing the boat across the choppy green water.

Yellow Dog sat in the bow, looking much calmer than Angus. McCormick smiled. There was something so right about a boy, his boat, and his dog. It had all been worth it — even the chickens.

Angus stopped to pinch himself as he packed his duffel bag. He could hardly believe that he and Dad were really leaving for the Winter Harbour trip the next day. Angus had looked forward to it for so long and now . . .

Silas sat on the floor of Angus' room. Actually, that night he was Lizard Man, in a green and red outfit that bagged at the knees. Beside Silas was the old-fashioned compass Angus and David had fished out of the harbor the day Silas had almost drowned. Under the compass was a nautical chart showing the west coast of nearby Vancouver Island.

Silas squinted at all the squiggly lines and tiny words. He didn't understand maps yet, but he thought they were kind of pretty, especially all the blue water.

Yellow Dog lay on the floor near Silas. He watched the little boy turn the compass dreamily around and around.

Angus cinched his duffel bag and kneeled down beside Lizard Man. He knew Silas was sad about not going on the trip too. But he'd have his turn. Maybe someday Angus and Silas would even be able to sail somewhere on their own.

Angus turned the compass so that north lined up with north on the chart and said, "Northeast. That's where we're going."

Silas tapped the compass' glass face and watched the magnetic needle twitch toward northeast before springing back to north. "See, it changes," said Silas.

Angus picked up the compass and looked at it. Who knew how long the thing had been sitting at the bottom of the sea. It seemed to work, but . . . Angus shook the compass and put it back down on the map. When he tapped it, the needle stayed steadily pointing north.

"It doesn't change. It works perfectly," Angus said.

Silas shrugged. "For you, maybe. When I do that it moves." Lizard Man stretched the sleeves of his costume to cover his small hands. "How come I can't go with you?" he asked, tapping the compass again.

Angus sighed. They'd been through this before. "Because you've got to deliver the papers and help Mom with the chickens while I'm gone."

Silas knew the truth. "I'm still not old enough, right?"

Angus suddenly realized how his father probably felt a lot of the time. It must be almost as hard to say "No" as it was to hear it — almost. "You're old enough, but, well . . ."

Angus didn't know what to say. Then he remembered what Dad always did in a pinch. Change the subject!

Angus snatched up the compass and handed it to Silas. "Here. You can keep this, okay? You practically died for it anyway."

Silas' eyes grew wide with wonder. The compass was a treasure as surely as anything discovered in a pirate's buried chest. Silas couldn't believe his brother would part with anything so precious. "I can? You don't want it back?"

Angus shook his head, even though he knew he could have sold the compass for some pretty good cash. It felt right to give the thing to Silas. "Nope. It's yours. Point it north and you'll know where I'm going."

Silas hugged the compass to his chest. The needle flipped around wildly. "Thanks, Angus." Lizard Man regarded his new possession with delighted awe.

Angus rose before dawn the next day. He'd almost been too excited to sleep. And when he had, he'd dreamed of the boat skimming the open sea.

Angus' life preserver glowed orange in the soft predawn light as he checked the lashing holding the boat to the *Cormorant's* stern. He wouldn't get to take the boat out until they reached Winter Harbour.

McCormick loaded the last of a dozen boxes of machine parts into the larger ship's hold. He felt tired from waking up so early, but almost as excited about the trip as Angus.

"Tofino, Yuquot, Winter Harbour," Katherine recited the itinerary, as if naming the *Cormorant's* destinations would make the trip go by faster.

"Three days, then two back," McCormick said. "I'll call at 7 A.M. every day."

Katherine nodded. She knew. They'd discussed the plans in detail many times. But repeating them was part of saying good-bye. Katherine hated saying good-bye to her husband, even though she sometimes enjoyed the peace and quiet when he was gone.

Electric Shock Man clutched his compass as he watched the activity on the dock. "It's the girl, back again," he reported.

Sara pedaled her bicycle down the dock. She said "Hi" to Angus at the very same time he said "Hi" to her.

"I thought I might have missed you," Sara said breathlessly. "Well, here, I made you these."

She handed Angus a heavy cookie tin. He popped the lid and looked inside. The aroma of blackened sugar reached his nostrils before he made sense of the contents. Darker dots in the hockey-puck sized briquettes tipped Angus off to the intended flavor: chocolate chip. He realized Sara was waiting for him to say something, so he stammered, "Thanks. Uh, thanks a lot."

"They're a little burned, but not much. The stove got out of control for a couple of minutes," said Sara. She was much better at baseball than baking, but she'd wanted to do something for Angus, to give him something to remember her by.

"They're, ah . . . thanks, anyway," Angus said.

"There's a lot of sugar and stuff — carbohydrates in them," Sara added. "If you're cold, they'll heat you up."

Angus looked at Sara and for a moment their eyes met like fingertips tentatively reaching for each other. Angus knew he should do or say something.

Should I kiss her? he wondered frantically, as the awkward silence stretched into an eternity. But Sara was his friend. What if . . .

The girl leaned toward Angus. Her lips pursed slightly, waiting to be kissed. But Angus was afraid. Without thinking, he backed away. His dark eyes still lingered on Sara's, but she broke the stare. The moment was lost.

"I'll see you when you get back," Sara said.

Angus nodded, then turned toward the boat.

Sara stood on the dock beside Katherine. They watched the *Cormorant* pull into the bay with the red boat on her stern. Angus and McCormick waved jauntily from the deck. Yellow Dog wagged his tail.

"See you in a week, guys. Good-bye, Yellow Dog," Katherine called. *Why am I saying good-bye to a dog?* she wondered.

Katherine still couldn't believe she'd fallen for the oldest trick in the book: "We'll just keep him until someone claims him." But even Katherine had to admit there was something about that Yellow Dog — something that made you notice him, something that made you say good-bye to him as if he could understand.

CHAPTER

6

ngus didn't remember the sun coming up over the land to the east. But dawn was always like that. One minute there was just that fuzzy white light, and the next thing you knew the sun was already up in the sky.

The *Cormorant* hugged the coast of Vancouver Island, which lay like a big green dragon on the right. To the left was the vast Pacific Ocean, stretching as far as the eye could see.

Angus felt the fresh salt breeze on his face as the *Cormorant* headed northwest between islands of arbutus shrubs and fir trees. The bushy arbutus bloomed with tiny white and pink flowers. In fall, there would be scarlet berries.

Yellow Dog stood beside Angus, his muzzle pointed into the wind that fluttered his velvety ears. Four strong paws steadied him on the rolling deck. Angus swallowed hard.

He felt his stomach lurch, but he convinced himself to ignore the queasy sensation. McCormick men didn't get seasick!

The wind rose as clouds crowded out the sun. The waves grew wilder, slapping at craggy cliffs as the *Cormorant* sailed by. White spray splashed against the gray sky.

Angus and Yellow Dog retreated down the companion-way steps into the cabin. Raindrops splattered on the windows. Angus held the ship's wheel while his father cooked over the small propane stove in the tidy galley.

The *Cormorant*'s cabin and lower deck, like those of all good ships, were fitted with every kind of necessity — and nothing extra. Cozy berths nestled the sides of the ship. Supplies were neatly stowed in the well-built lockers.

Two survival suits hung in packs on the cabin bulkhead beside the Navigation Station and the Emergency Position Indicating Radio Beacon, or EPIRB, required by the Coast Guard on every ship.

Angus liked how everything on a ship had special names. The cabin floor wasn't just the floor, but the *sole*. Left wasn't plain old left, it was *port*, and right was *starboard*. The front of the ship was the *bow*, and the rear the *stern*.

The *Cormorant* was *shipshape*, but one of its passengers wasn't. Yellow Dog swayed on the pitching sole. His brown eyes rolled miserably. A low, whining moan escaped his muzzle — quickly followed by breakfast.

"Oh, no!" McCormick exclaimed.

The *Cormorant* sheltered in a quiet cove overnight.

McCormick looked at his watch to know when it was morning. The overcast day dripping with light rain was not much different from night. The *Cormorant* was alone in the foggy morning, as if it was the only ship in the world, and McCormick and his son the only people. Angus slept in the rear of the cabin with Yellow Dog sprawled on top of him.

McCormick was glad when his watch read seven. Now he had an excuse to use the radio to call Katherine — and make sure the outside world really did exist. Static crackled, then he heard Katherine's voice.

"It's cold, wet, gray," McCormick reported.

His wife's voice sounded tinny on the radio's speaker. "Too bad. It's great here. How are the guys?"

McCormick glanced back at his sleeping son. Yellow Dog's ears had lifted at the sound of the radio, but the dog hadn't moved. "They're great."

"We already miss you," Katherine added.

McCormick smiled. Going away was always fun; coming home would be even better.

There was no point waiting out the weather, which had no intention of changing — except for the worse. So McCormick took the *Cormorant* back out on the churning sea.

Hard rain splattered the cabin windows, like the insistent fingers of a visitor tapping to gain entrance. Huge swells lifted the ship, then dropped it down again in gaping valleys of black water. The horizon, and everything between, was gray. So much for their pleasant cruise. At least Yellow Dog didn't get sick again.

The next morning found the *Cormorant* in a sheltered inlet near the remains of a dilapidated fishing dock. In the gray light of another rainy dawn, Angus watched his father plot the *Cormorant*'s position on a chart.

"We pass Yuquot, then it's Kyuquot . . ." McCormick's hand drew a quick clean line across the map from one harbor town to the next along Vancouver Island's mountainous western coast.

Angus wondered if he would ever be that confident, that sure of his own skill. He hoped so!

"I think we'll make Catala Island in about three hours," McCormick continued. "We can wait out the weather there, before it gets dark."

He handed the ruler and pencil to Angus, who carefully drew the line to Catala Island.

"There won't be any stars tonight," Angus ventured.

"Right," McCormick said. The boy would make a sailor yet! He had all the right instincts — and the love of the sea.

The *Cormorant* held a steady northwest course across the choppy Pacific. Its rising and falling stern pointed at a gray horizon split by sudden lightning. The McCormicks were too far away to hear the accompanying thunder. But the silent flashes were just as terrible without its boom.

McCormick's neck and shoulders tensed as he struggled to hold the wheel steady. Though it made him slightly dizzy, Angus studied the map. He braced himself against the heaving table, looked out the window, then back at the map. "Dad."

McCormick peered through the rain and saw a flashing

beacon perhaps two miles away. "Yuquot lighthouse. Nootka Island," he observed.

Angus was happy. He had figured their position correctly. "So it's about an hour to Catala Island?" An hour of this churning sounded like an awfully long time!

McCormick shook his head. He wished! The storm was moving quicker than he had estimated. He didn't want to worry Angus, but they could be in for a rough time. "A little longer than that. We should stop sooner."

McCormick turned the dials of the ship's radio and picked up the handset. Getting through to anyone was getting harder by the minute.

For a terrifying moment the *Cormorant* was completely submerged as she crashed through a wave. Angus felt his stomach lurch as his world turned sideways, then righted itself.

What if it doesn't come up after the next roll? Angus wondered. Yellow Dog whimpered. Petting the dog to comfort him made Angus feel better — but not much.

The storm came closer and closer, until Angus could not only hear the thunder but felt as if it were ripping through him like heavy-metal music. What had passed for daylight was fading fast, dissolved in sheets of gray rain. Angus noticed that the *Cormorant*'s instrument panel was glowing now.

Will we find shelter before dark? Angus wondered. He swallowed hard and tried to take comfort in the sight of his father standing tall at the ship's wheel.

McCormick's deep voice shouted into the radio. "*Cormorant* calling Tofino Coast Guard radio."

Angus was relieved to hear the swift reply through the static. "Tofino Coast Guard radio . . ."

If they said more, Angus only heard static. Then the Coast Guard radioman's voice said, "*Cormorant*, go ahead with your position."

Static filled the cabin. McCormick punched buttons. The Coast Guard radioman's voice came and went, like a distant ghost calling on the wind.

McCormick shouted, not knowing whether his message would be received or not. "Tofino, we're off northern Nootka Island, roughly two hours past Yuquot. Do you have the weather forecast for the next few hours and overnight?"

Words punctuated the static. But Angus and his father could not understand any of them. McCormick looked through the cabin's front window at a boiling sea of twelve-foot waves. There was no point in panicking, but that didn't stop his heart from beating double-time.

McCormick switched the radio off, then on again. "*Cormorant* calling Tofino Coast Guard radio."

More garbled words interrupted the steady static. McCormick hung up the handset and switched off the radio. They were on their own.

"Never trust the ocean, Angus," McCormick warned.

"Don't worry," Angus replied.

McCormick felt proud of having fathered such a brave boy. "Let's just put into shore and throw the anchor out."

The ship might get smashed to bits, but at least they'd be close to land.

"Yeah, let's," Angus agreed hastily. Shore had never sounded quite so good before.

"Get the chart, we'll find a landing," McCormick

instructed, giving the wheel a sharp turn. Through the haze of rain and gloom, he could just make out the contours of land about three miles away.

Three miles can take a long time to cross when the sea is raging. Waves like giant angry fists pounded the *Cormorant*'s sides.

McCormick and Angus suddenly found themselves thrown against the wall. When the ship righted herself once more, they were tossed on the floor. They flew from one end of the cabin to the other, helpless as rag dolls. A series of savage waves rocked the ship, each one bigger than the last.

Angus' shins bounced on the deck, hard. He couldn't regain his feet and wasn't sure he should try. Amid the noisy storm, Angus heard the creaking of the *Cormorant*'s boards, as if the ship might break apart at any second.

Angus told himself it was a solid ship. But nothing felt solid right then. The boy could barely tell up from down. His teeth rattled in his skull, and his heart pounded like the thunder shaking the sky.

One second, he saw the angry gray sky outside the cabin's windows. The next, the glass was filled with the bubbling, foaming sea.

Yellow Dog slid backwards across the floor into the ship's galley. Water spurted through cracks in the wall above him.

Everything that wasn't nailed down flew through the air: cups, plates, pots, pans, sugar, tea, maps, charts, pencils, and rulers blew from one end of the cabin to the other in a rain of clutter. The flame on the small propane stove started to burn.

Another wave crashed into the ship, tearing at the cabin door and smashing the windows. The stove hissed with flammable gas. Its hungry flame shot toward the scattered charts and kitchen debris — and a fire was born!

McCormick pulled himself up and grabbed his son. How had this happened? Their father-son cruise was rapidly turning into a major disaster!

"Angus!" McCormick screamed.

"I'm okay, Dad!" Angus shouted over the din.

McCormick knew seconds could count in a situation like this, so he swiftly tied a rope around Angus and held tight to the other end. McCormick reached for the survival suit packs hanging on the bulkhead, but they were just beyond his grasp.

Before McCormick could move, the *Cormorant* was slapped by another wave that turned it around completely and submerged it in roiling water. The shock knocked father and son off their feet. Yellow Dog barked, trying to reach them from across the cabin, nails scrabbling for a hold on the tilted deck.

The *Cormorant* bent toward the waves at a forty-five degree angle. McCormick reached for the engine controls and jammed the throttle. Just then, the ship was lifted by another huge wave off the stern, which slammed the bow into the sea. The wheel spun crazily for a moment, then the rudder snapped.

Dark smoke billowed from the galley. There was no time. "Get on the upper deck, Angus! Get the raft, go on!" McCormick cried.

"Yellow Dog!" Angus cried.

McCormick hit the EPIRB switch on the wall-mounted, hand-held PLB NAV station. The red light came on as he lifted it out of its holder. *It's working!* McCormick thought gratefully. At least their distress signal would go out before the ship went down.

But even as he took comfort from the red light's glow, it winked out again. McCormick punched it once, then harder. But the light did not reappear. It was dead.

By then the small fire in the galley had blossomed into a full-blown blaze. McCormick's face felt scorched from the heat of it as he grabbed a fire extinguisher. He aimed the nozzle at the wild, crackling heart of the flames, but it was too late. The fire was eating the ship's wooden insides, and at the rate it was spreading there would soon be nothing left.

McCormick furiously flung the extinguisher at the flames. Then he turned to Angus who was clinging to the deck, trying to reach the life raft canister.

Another wave slammed into the ship. And as the wave returned to the surging sea, it dragged the life raft canister with it. Angus felt the deck disappear beneath him. He was floating. He was moving!

Without thinking, his grip tightened. He clung in blind desperation, until he felt the solid deck beneath him once more.

McCormick clutched the other end of Angus' lifeline as he crawled toward the stern. "The boat! Angus! Get to your boat. I'll hold you!"

With the life raft gone, Angus' red boat was their only hope. If the boy could just get it into the water before the *Cormorant* sank . . .

Angus clawed his way to the stern where his red boat

thrashed at the end of its line. Yellow Dog followed Angus, nails hanging onto the deck for dear life.

McCormick held the rope and braced himself against the deck. He didn't pray exactly. He just thought with all his might, *Please let Angus reach the red boat! Please let us live through this storm!*

And then the propane tank in the galley finally exploded in a terrific burst of flame. Angus had to reach the red boat or they had no chance at all. Though it frightened him to do so, McCormick inched along the cabin's door frame, loosened the lifeline, hoping to give Angus enough slack to reach the boat.

Angus held the red boat's tie line, but when he tried to pull it near to the *Cormorant*, the waves pulled it away. Angus knew he couldn't win a tug-of-war with the sea. "Dad, I can't get it in! It won't come!"

"Cut it loose!" McCormick cried. If the *Cormorant* sank, and it surely would soon, he didn't want the red boat pulled down with it.

Angus fumbled for his grandfather's knife and managed to cut the taut rope. A twenty-foot wave washed over the *Cormorant*, tearing wood in its wake.

Angus' lifeline suddenly sped through McCormick's hands, burning his skin as it went. McCormick was tossed toward the bow, away from his son.

Angus spiraled into the freezing water, followed by Yellow Dog. For a few awful moments, Angus was completely lost in the cold, bubbling sea. Then his head bobbed to the foamy surface, eyes stinging with salt water and mouth gasping for air. One hand clutched the knife, the other the line to the red boat.

Angus' shivering fingers managed to put the knife in his pocket. Then he struggled to swim closer to the boat. Angus felt a tug on his life preserver. Yellow Dog was attempting another watery rescue. But the powerful Labrador was having a hard time keeping his own head above the wild waves.

Finally, Angus reached the red boat. He held onto it desperately with one hand and Yellow Dog's collar with the other. Angus looked across the churning sea and saw the flames on the *Cormorant* climbing defiantly into the sky.

"DAAAAAD!" Angus screamed so hard he felt as if he'd torn his throat open. But the rain, wind, and smashing waves made Angus' voice sound faint — even to him.

McCormick clambered to the uppermost side of the capsizing *Cormorant*. The fire thrived despite the violent rain. Balancing precariously on the burning wreckage, McCormick searched for his son and the bright red boat.

"AAANNNGUUUSS!" McCormick's anguished cry was swallowed by the sea. His eyes strained, but found no sign of boy or boat.

Angus pulled himself and Yellow Dog onto the red boat, which was sloshing with water. He realized, dimly, that the boat was drifting away from the *Cormorant*. But there was nothing Angus could do, even if he could have reached his father's burning ship.

Angus saw the column of orange flame writhing against the dusky sky. The *Cormorant* looked small and terribly far away.

"DAD!" Angus screamed futilely. Then the horrible sight was blotted out by a wall of water crashing it down into the sea.

Panic seized Angus. His father was gone! And he was alone, more terribly alone than he ever imagined he could be. The last light of day faded from the sky, and with it the last of the exhausted boy's courage.

Angus hadn't cried for a long time, not like the way he'd cried at Silas' age. But when darkness made it impossible to keep searching for his father, Angus collapsed on the deck and sobbed.

CHAPTER

7

 atherine snapped awake as soon as she heard the phone ring. "Hi, McCormick," she said groggily.

But the man who answered wasn't McCormick.

"Hello, Katherine. It's John Gale. I'm sorry to wake you." McCormick's friend was calling from the Rescue Coordination Center's office in Victoria.

Katherine felt sleepy and confused. But a growing sense of alarm was jolting her awake faster than any coffee. "John? What is it?"

"Well, we had an indication that *Cormorant* might have had a problem . . ." Gale began.

Katherine felt her stomach sink to her toes. "Are they okay?"

Gale took a moment to recover from his disappointment. It hadn't been logical, really, to expect her to say, "Hold on a minute, I'll let you ask McCormick yourself." And yet, Gale had hoped, somehow, that McCormick and Angus had made it home. Gale realized he'd better answer quickly, or risk worrying Katherine.

"They'll be tied up in a shelter somewhere," he said, hoping he sounded confident.

Just then, Coast Guard officer Jankovic handed Gale a computer printout. Gale scanned the sheet as he said, "Equatorial I.D. Satellite picked up an EPIRB, so we've started harbor checks. We know they were on the radio a few hours ago."

Silas came into his parents' bedroom, rubbing the sleep from his eyes. "What's wrong, Mom?" He could tell she wasn't talking to Dad, and who else would call so early?

Katherine tried to keep her voice calm as she concluded her conversation with Gale, "Call me as soon as you can."

Katherine couldn't let Silas know she was scared. But she was very frightened.

Gale was glad to hang up the phone. Katherine's anxiety had been almost tangible, and he needed to keep a clear head. Gale turned to Jankovic.

"Tofino has been calling on 22 Alpha without response," the officer reported.

"Start a GMB, communications search," Gale commanded. "Where are the aircraft?"

Jankovic replied, "They should be in the zone, sir."

By sunrise, a Buffalo aircraft out of the Canadian Air Force 442 Squadron was roaring over the deep forest of Nootka Island. The thick carpet of green stretched from

one end of the island to the other and was surrounded by the vast Pacific Ocean. The plane roared on, between tall thunderheads, dropping below the low ceiling of mist. And everywhere was the same green sea.

Angus watched the green waves smash savagely against black rocks as the tide crept up the shore. A strong wind ruffled clumps of seaweed on the sandy beach of a tiny inlet. Beyond the sand was the endless forest. No sign of human life broke the monotony of that perfect wilderness.

Angus poked a stick into the frigid water, trying to snare his orange life jacket. But the greedy waves sucked it out to sea, along with several boards from the red boat.

Angus turned away in disgust and walked back to the ruins of the boat. After all his careful work, the red boat had been badly smashed against the rocky inlet.

Angus had propped the boat upside-down on chunks of driftwood and rocks well up from the high-tide mark. He had covered its broken sides with more driftwood to make a shelter from rain and wind. A plastic tarp door completed his home.

Angus reached inside his pocket and pulled out the silver dog whistle. His parched lips and tired lungs still managed to produce the beautiful tone.

Yellow Dog trotted up the beach from the other direction. Angus added another piece of driftwood to his shelter and folded the tarp as the dog drew near.

Angus patted the soft yellow head. "I really hope Dad didn't get hurt, Yellow."

The dog settled down at Angus' feet with his head between his paws.

"I don't want him to be hurt," Angus said, hoping he wouldn't cry again.

The day passed very slowly for Angus and Yellow Dog. Despair lapped at the edges of Angus' mind, like a rising tide. Whenever he found the strength he tried to do something constructive. He rigged a clothesline on which to dry his wet clothes. Then, wrapped in his tarp, Angus carefully laid out the contents of his camping kit on the sand. *This is what Dad would do,* Angus decided. *He'd see what he had to work with and make plans for what to do next.*

Being all by himself, Angus had quickly fallen into the habit of talking out loud to Yellow Dog. It was better than the awful silence, and Yellow Dog gave a good impression of understanding.

"Tin of biscuits," Angus began listing his worldly goods. He checked the tin and said, "Broken open. A flashlight, no good. Two boxes of matches . . ."

Angus examined the contents of the soggy cartons. A few of the matches looked as if they might still light. Yellow Dog watched the boy's every move.

"Some of them are okay," Angus reported.

Yellow Dog looked thoughtful. Angus continued, "Fishing line and hooks. Some dry packaged stuff. The cooking kit. No gas. And Sara's cookies. No dog food," Angus concluded sadly.

Then he opened the cookie tin, pulled out one of the dry, black "pucks" and bit it. Angus felt a shock of pain travel up his jaw. He'd almost broken a tooth!

Maybe there was some dog food after all. Angus held

the cookie out to Yellow Dog, who greedily snapped it up in his strong, white teeth.

Seconds later, the dog spat out the black disk. Angus picked it up and was about to pitch it into the sea, when he stopped himself. "We might get really hungry," he explained to the dog.

Yellow Dog looked at him. Longing animated his dark eyes.

"I know. I *am* hungry," Angus agreed.

While Angus and Yellow Dog contemplated Sara's cookies, the Buffalo plane roared up the coastline. It banked sharply and circled a barely submerged reef. Smashed by swirling waves and clinging to the rocks was the burned-out shell of the *Cormorant*. The pilot jettisoned a life-raft pack and smoke flares from the plane's rear door.

Following the flares and the Buffalo's position report, a Labrador helicopter was soon hovering over the wreckage. Rotors flattened a circle of water beneath the aircraft. A SARTECH (Search and Rescue Technician) was lowered on a cable to examine the swamped craft. A second SARTECH dropped to the reef.

The SARTECHs found McCormick cocooned in his survival suit and a plastic sheet. One rescuer touched McCormick's bruised face, looking for a sign of life. McCormick's eyes fluttered open.

"Did you find my boy?" he croaked through swollen lips. Worry over Angus had flooded McCormick's mind even before he was fully awake. Then came the pain in his burned hands, which felt like they had been scraped by a cheese grater.

The SARTECH shook his head. They hadn't found the boy yet.

"I'm here to help you," he said. "Let's see if you're okay."

McCormick didn't care. "He's in his boat. It's red and white."

The SARTECH smiled reassuringly. "We'll find him. Was there anyone else?"

"His dog was with him," McCormick said.

Yellow Dog was with Angus as he furiously stabbed at the sand with a stick. Finally, Angus dug up a clam! He tucked his treasure in his cook pot, along with a large handful of seaweed. Yellow Dog snatched another clam in his jaws and ran off along the rocky beach.

By the time Angus tried his hand at fishing, the sun had nearly left the sky. An orange reflection winked off the surface of the silver whistle, which now hung on a string around Angus' neck.

The boy balanced carefully on a seaweed-covered rock that jutted into the ocean. He dangled his fishing line in one hand and waited for the spiny rock cod to swallow the hook. Angus knew the fish, despite its ugly appearance, would be good eating. His mouth watered and his fingers shook.

And suddenly the line came to life in Angus' hands. The cod was hooked! Angus pulled it up onto the rocks. Yellow Dog barked at the frantically flopping fish.

Angus put his foot across the fish's body. He felt pity for the cod's desperate struggle. But the thought of his catch escaping back into the sea was more than the hungry boy could bear.

Finally, the fish stopped moving. Angus pulled out his knife and cut it across the throat.

"Sorry, fish," Angus said softly. Then he freed the hook from the cod's mouth and carefully folded it up with the fishing line. Yellow Dog whined hungrily.

Angus carried the fish back to his shelter, which now boasted a driftwood front door. He piled rocks to form a windbreak and a chimney, then started a fire the way Dad had showed him.

Angus struggled to swallow the lump that clogged his throat whenever he thought of his father. All that first day, Angus kept expecting that somehow his father would walk down the beach to greet him. But when it didn't happen, when it kept not happening, Angus' sadness deepened. The only way to cope with it was by not letting himself think about his father at all. And that was impossible.

Angus fed the fire with pieces of driftwood and slivers of the red boat. It was hard to believe that the boat, which had meant so much to him for so long, was now just fuel to fry an ugly fish.

Yellow Dog stared at the fish frying in the metal mess-kit pan. Angus almost laughed at the dog's intent expression — as if all the treasure and great secrets of the world were contained in that sizzling pan.

The yellow muzzle inched closer. The black nostrils flared to better inhale the smoky fumes. Long strands of drool dripped from Yellow Dog's mouth. Angus had to keep moving the pan to stop the dog's slobber from saucing the fish.

Angus tossed a handful of lichen into the boiling water in the cook pot. "I'm saving the freeze-dried vegetables," he explained.

Yellow Dog listened patiently, but his eyes never left the frying fish. Angus watched more drool come out of the furry muzzle.

"I think it's a little small in here for both of us," Angus said. But Yellow Dog didn't take the hint. Instead, he edged in even closer.

CHAPTER

8

ilas couldn't eat his supper, and Katherine couldn't blame him. A tight knot of worry filled her stomach too, and it didn't seem to leave any room for food.

When the phone rang, Katherine lunged for it. She spoke into the receiver almost before her hand had brought it to her mouth. "Yes?"

Silas watched his mother's face as she listened to the person at the other end of the phone. Her pinched mouth softened. Her eyes filled with tears.

"Yes! Yes, I'll be there in the morning, John," Katherine said. She wiped away tears as she hung up the phone. Then she turned to Silas and asked, "Do you want to go see Dad?"

"What about Angus and Yellow?" Silas demanded.

Katherine looked into her son's eyes. What could she say to him? Joy and sorrow were tugging her heart in two.

The next morning, pilot Jeremy Cooper picked up Katherine and Silas in his float plane. They soon arrived at the government dock in Tofino, a fishing town near Clayoquot Sound. John Gale had set up his search headquarters in an abandoned fish-packing plant near the docks.

Gale and a nurse escorted Katherine down a hall in the Tofino Hospital. Katherine was weak from worry and relief. She hadn't looked in a mirror for days, and that was just as well.

When McCormick suddenly appeared around a corner, Katherine's red eyes gushed with still more tears. She ran across the polished floor into his eager arms. Her mouth found his in a long grateful kiss. He was here! He was really here! Scraped up and knocked around, but in one piece! Tears poured from McCormick's eyes too.

"He got in the boat," McCormick said by way of greeting. "He got in the boat all right, and he had the life jacket on."

Katherine held her husband's face between her hands as if to make sure it was real. "They'll find him, McCormick. Don't worry. They'll find him."

Katherine believed in miracles now. After all, weren't McCormick's strong arms around her once again?

Silas hugged the old marine compass. He was dressed in a red cape, with green and black accessories, but Katherine didn't remember who he was supposed to be. There wasn't room in her mind for much beyond McCORMICK IS ALIVE and please, God, let Angus be too!

Silas looked at his father and declared, "We'll find him, Dad."

As the sun set, Katherine felt as if her heart was also sinking. Each minute of the day had been filled with hope, and now day was giving in to night and the terrible despair. *What if they didn't find Angus?* Katherine couldn't stand the horrible possibility, and she couldn't stop considering it, either.

Wanting to stay close to John Gale's office, the McCormicks decided to check into a nearby motel. Gale unloaded their bags from his car while McCormick handed the desk clerk his credit card.

"That's all right, Mr. McCormick. We'll worry about that some other time," the clerk said.

The wreck of the *Cormorant* had been all over the local news. And the story had touched the hearts of everyone in the small, isolated community. Not charging for the rooms was the only thing the clerk could do to express his sympathy.

When John Gale rejoined them, Katherine asked, "Do they search at night?"

Gale tipped his head toward the window. Rain slid down the glass. The light from the motel sign was muffled by a curtain of fog. "Yes, but night vision and the other tech stuff are not that effective in this weather."

Gale saw the corners of Katherine's mouth dip. "Don't worry," he hastened to assure her. "It's been only two days. I'm sure he'll still be floating around in that little boat."

CHAPTER

9

he next day, Angus smashed what was left of his boat and piled it into a six-foot-high pyramid of wood. His stomach growled with hunger. Fish, sea urchins, and a few precious vegetables had not made much of an impression on his stomach. As he'd told Yellow Dog, "Not a lot of calories, I don't think."

Angus wasn't accustomed to thinking about calories. But food meant a lot more to Angus now that there was less of it. He slumped down beside the signal fire and filled himself with happy thoughts about lighting it, and being rescued, and chomping into the biggest hamburger in the world.

Angus was bored, so he rolled chunks of bull kelp into homemade baseballs. He whacked at the balls with a driftwood bat. Yellow Dog retrieved the shaggy brown balls. It was fun!

Angus thought of playing baseball with Silas, David, and Sara. He would love telling them about this once he was rescued. *If he was rescued* . . . Angus whacked another baseball and tried to hang onto the happy feeling, but it was gone.

When they tired of their game, Angus and Yellow Dog slept in the hot sun. Yellow Dog stretched out on his back, with his four legs pointing at the blue sky. Angus scratched Yellow's warm furry belly, then fell back to sleep.

Unfortunately, not every day was sunny. When the rain poured outside, Angus and Yellow Dog huddled miserably in their shelter. Angus cut pieces of his precious tarp to make himself a new pair of shoes that he tied to his cold feet with rope.

He used his knife to shave a few bits of boat wood into slivers. Then he refilled his kindling bag, which was made from another piece of tarp. Keeping the waterproof bag full of dry kindling meant Angus could start a fire any time he needed.

"You always have to work toward the next day," he told Yellow Dog. "They could come anytime, you know. I know that. You know that. And they will. We both know that, but we've got to be prepared just in case it takes them another couple of days to get here. So now we have enough kindling . . . just till they get here. I mean, that's all we'll need, right?"

Yellow Dog's large brown eyes seemed to agree. Angus carefully sealed the kindling bag.

Before he put away his knife, Angus carved a small notch on a stick. It was the fifth notch, for the fifth day Angus and Yellow Dog had been on their own.

A sound like the buzzing of an enormous bee invaded Angus' dream. He swatted at the bee, but the sound only grew louder. Angus sat up. Yellow Dog's jaws snapped at the invisible intruder.

Only then did Angus realize the buzz was not from a bee. The sound was coming from a plane engine! Angus' heart fluttered. This was it!

"The signal fire!" he said frantically.

Angus snatched up his kindling bag and tore out of the shelter. His sleepy feet stumbled over rocks, but he was too busy to feel the pain.

When he reached the pyramid of wood, Angus fumbled for a match. He struck it, but failed to protect the flame. The match went out.

Angus took a deep breath and focused on keeping the next match lit. Cupping his hand around the fragile yellow flame, he held it against a scrap of driftwood. He sighed with relief when the wood caught, but was disappointed to see how slowly it spread.

Angus and Yellow Dog scanned the dawn sky for the plane. They couldn't see it anywhere, but they definitely heard the engine's loud roar. Angus grinned. *They'd come at last! He was going to be rescued! And these five lonely, terrifying days would soon be just a story to tell his friends back home.*

Angus watched a small spiral of gray smoke rise from the fire. *Come on! Come on!* But the fire took its own time growing.

Yellow Dog looked at Angus, and Angus looked at Yellow Dog as the horrible truth became clear. The engine sound was fading. The plane was leaving!

Would it circle back? Angus wondered. Panic gripped him. *It had to! It just had to! But . . . what if it didn't?*

Angus listened intently. The sound was faint now and growing fainter by the minute. NO!

Angus felt the heat of the signal fire warming his skin. He watched the flames bitterly. He had burned his carefully constructed pyramid for nothing.

Angus could barely move for the rest of that day. Things had been bad enough before the plane had come and gone, but now he felt more frightened and alone than ever. Yellow Dog seemed in the same downcast state.

Together, they stared out at the ocean and watched the big orange sun sink toward the blue horizon. The orange disk was so far away. Everything was far away.

Behind them, the signal fire burned down. Angus rose wearily to his feet. He dragged a piece of driftwood to the fire.

While Angus watched the flickering flames, Yellow Dog wandered up the beach. Angus heard a wolf howl. Its hollow call echoed throughout the dark green wall of trees that bordered the beach. Angus did not like looking into the forest. In some ways it seemed even deeper than the green ocean.

"Here boy!" Angus shouted, though his voice was hoarse and faint. "Yellow, let's get inside. Here boy."

When the dog did not come immediately, Angus felt a stab of panic. Then he remembered the whistle hanging on the string around his neck. Angus blew into the whistle and heard its sweet tone. Yellow Dog came trotting down the beach, tail wagging.

While Angus and Yellow Dog comforted each other inside their shelter, several miles away a formation of three Beaver float planes buzzed the coastline. A quarter of a mile of darkening sky separated each plane, which banked and turned inland.

McCormick rode in one of the civilian craft that had volunteered to join the search for his son.

"It'll be completely dark in ten minutes," the pilot told McCormick. "We've got to go back in."

McCormick reluctantly lowered binoculars from his bloodshot eyes. He reminded himself that Vancouver Island was 279 miles long, with 12,408 square miles of endless green forest. McCormick nodded wearily, then drained the dregs of a cold cup of coffee.

That night, McCormick drank more coffee in the search headquarters at the old fish-packing plant. The coffee was hot and fresh, but he didn't notice the difference. The last of the tired searchers wandered in from the dock, then took their leave.

"We've got more planes working further south and east," John Gale told McCormick and Katherine.

Silas sat at a table watching his compass and only half-listening to the adults.

"East? You mean inland?" Katherine didn't bother hiding her alarm.

"A little, but the coastline mostly, for now," Gale replied. "We flew it right away, six days ago. Then every day at different times we've gone over it."

"He's with the boat," said McCormick. "He wouldn't

leave it. He'll be with the boat." McCormick wished he felt as certain as he sounded. Since the storm, nothing seemed as certain as before.

"It's a really good boat," Silas piped up. "Angus built it with Dad."

Katherine sat down beside Silas. With everyone so worried about Angus, she was concerned that her youngest was getting lost in the shuffle. She watched Silas turn the old compass slowly, and wondered how much of what was happening the little boy understood.

"If the boat didn't sink, we'll find it," Gale assured his friend.

McCormick sighed. "But a boy in a life jacket may be more difficult. You can fly over him and not see him. Is that what you're saying, John? I mean it's possible we might not see him?"

Gale didn't know what to say. He was torn between wanting to make McCormick feel better and knowing that tough truths would have to be faced sooner or later. "We never stop a search, McCormick, if there's any hope. You know that."

There was nothing to do but go back to the motel. But each night felt like defeat. McCormick moved slowly, feeling like a very old man.

"Please don't stop looking for him, John," Katherine pleaded.

Gale looked her squarely in the eyes and said, "I won't stop looking, Katherine."

She clung to his promise. She hoped it would be enough to get her through the night. "We should be getting back to the motel."

Gale nodded. "I'll come and get you guys at eight o'clock."

Though his parents were ready to leave, Silas lingered at the table, still looking at his compass. He had lined up north on the compass' bearing line with north on Angus' crumpled chart. The card wobbled under the glass.

"That's weird," Silas said.

The adults turned to look at Silas.

"The compass. It's pointing south now."

McCormick was too tired to explain compasses to Silas again. The old thing was probably broken anyway. But if Silas wanted to cling to it as the last thing Angus had given to him, McCormick couldn't argue with that. He held out his arms to the little boy and scooped him up. "Come on Si, let's go."

CHAPTER

10

y dawn, Angus' signal fire was little more than a wisp of smoke among the ashes. He poked at it with a piece of wood. Angus heard a yelp and turned. Yellow Dog stiffened.

Angus looked at the figure down the shore, a dark silhouette against the pinkish sky. The four-legged shape looked like Yellow Dog. And yet . . . Angus felt the hairs on the back of his neck prickle. He squinted and distinctly felt the animal looking back at him. This was a wild creature completely at home in this wild place.

Angus felt like a caged canary being stalked by a cat. With a quick stab of fear, Angus realized the visitor was a wolf!

For a moment, Angus might have been a caveman. There was no rescue plane. There was no world beyond that lonely stretch of beach and woods. And there wasn't even a stout club in his hand. There was only fear.

Then the wolf turned and sauntered into the woods. Angus hurried back to the shelter, glad of Yellow Dog's company. He didn't want to admit, even to himself, how much the wolf's presence unnerved him.

To calm himself, Angus decided to take stock of his remaining supplies. He spread the tarp on the shelter floor and carefully brushed away the sand.

Angus counted fifty-three matches, the tarp bag full of kindling, his yellow nylon rope, canteen, and the tin of Sara's cookies. A wave of despair washed over him.

Angus suddenly thought of Robinson Crusoe. How convenient to have an entire wrecked ship at your disposal. Angus, on the other hand, had little more than burnt cookies. It was pathetic. His was going to be an awfully short story if he didn't do something fast.

Angus pressed his lips together in a determined grimace. He bundled up his worldly goods inside the tarp. He tied it into a pack with the rope and slung it over his shoulder. He stooped to fill his canteen from a puddle of rain water.

Angus tied a piece of tarp to the top of an oar. He stuck the handle in the sand, then stacked rocks around his makeshift flag to keep it upright.

With a piece of charcoal from the burnt-out signal fire, the boy wrote a message on the oar's wide blade: WALKING SOUTH, ANGUS.

Then he and Yellow Dog faced south. To the left was the endless green wall of the forest. To the right, the endless green sea. Yellow Dog grumbled. His brown eyes looked worried as they contemplated Angus' chosen path.

"We've been here too long," the boy explained. "They're

not coming, Yellow. The Yuquot lighthouse is south. We passed it I think two or three hours before we wrecked."

Yellow Dog gave a thoughtful huff.

"There will be someone at the lighthouse," Angus said.

Yellow Dog listened.

"It can't be too far. Maybe fifteen miles," the boy estimated. "We can make it. We can find the lighthouse."

Yellow Dog barked, as if to say, *Where you go, I go.*

While Angus and Yellow Dog began their long march, the other McCormicks started their day in the Blue Vista Motel. Silas put down his old compass long enough to pull on his Electric Shock Man costume.

Katherine called into the bathroom where the water had been running for a long time. "McCormick? You ready?"

There was no answer. Katherine opened the door. She saw her husband standing over a sink brimming with hot water. The mirror was completely fogged with steam. McCormick's red-rimmed eyes stared into the mirror, unseeing.

The razor jumped in his shaky hand. When he pressed it to his lathered neck, scarlet blood stained the white shaving cream. But McCormick took no notice.

"McCormick! Honey, look what you're doing!" Katherine cried. "Here . . ."

She turned off the water and pressed a washcloth against his bleeding neck. When he faced her, tears poured from his eyes.

"I lost my boy," McCormick murmured.

Katherine had never seen her husband like this, not even when his father had died.

"Listen to me," she began gently. But McCormick seemed miles away, lost in his grief.

"McCormick, *listen* to me!" Katherine repeated in the tone she used for scolding the boys. "You're not doing him any good standing here falling apart. Are you?"

McCormick's slumped shoulders straightened. Katherine was right. He had to be strong for her . . . and Angus.

"We're not alone in this," Katherine said.

McCormick didn't understand. "What do you mean?" he asked.

Katherine didn't bother answering. She just pressed a Band-aid on his nick and brought him outside where John Gale was waiting.

When they reached search headquarters, McCormick blinked in disbelief. The old fish plant was packed with people. More civilian volunteers mobbed the entrance trying to get inside.

Gale led the McCormicks through the crowded parking lot. Friends and acquaintances waved to the worried couple and shouted encouragement. Some clapped McCormick on the back or shook his hand.

McCormick didn't remember the name of the man whose face was suddenly in front of his.

"We'll find him," the man said warmly.

McCormick's eyes misted with tears. "Thank you," he whispered thickly, before following Katherine and Gale into the office.

McCormick's eyes widened when he saw the bright orange object on the chair beside the cluttered table serving as Gale's desk. Gale followed the direction of his friend's gaze. "It was found some distance from the wreck site, and it may not be his," Gale cautioned.

McCormick and Katherine examined the life jacket. McCormick remembered the day he'd bought it at the hardware store.

"It's his," McCormick asserted. "He's on the shore."

Gale was skeptical. "We've crossed and recrossed the shore."

Katherine somehow knew her husband was correct. "McCormick's right. I think he's on shore."

Gale knew how people got in situations like this. They clung to hope until they absolutely had to give it up. But Gale himself was no quitter. "Don't worry. We're not stopping," he assured the McCormicks.

Silas looked thoughtful, then remarked, "I think he might be on Jupiter."

Katherine hugged Silas close. This was all so strange for him, so hard to understand. What would they do if Silas had to learn to live without his big brother? Katherine tightened her hold around Silas before finally releasing him. She knew if she held him any longer, she would start to cry again.

John Gale produced a toy Coast Guard boat from his pocket. Silas happily accepted the toy and immediately started to play with it. The boat was going to Jupiter to bring Angus home.

Gale knew what he had to say next, but he couldn't look into his friend's eyes. "If he's not on shore, I'm afraid I have to tell you that officially our point of reasonable chance of survival has gone by."

Silas looked up from his new toy. "Yellow will save him."

McCormick looked at Gale. If anyone else had said that, he might have raged at him. But McCormick trusted Gale like a brother.

"It's okay," he said softly. But it wasn't. Nothing would be okay until they found his son.

At that moment, his son and Yellow Dog were picking their way south along a jagged, rocky shore. The midday sun beat down on the boy's back as he crossed a fjord surrounded by steep cliffs. The rugged terrain of rocks crusted with barnacles and shells was visible through the shallow water of low tide. With his four strong paws, Yellow Dog had no trouble keeping up with the boy.

Suddenly, the dog's yellow ears twitched. Then Angus heard the sound too. It was a plane!

Angus splashed frantically through the water. He looked up and saw the Beaver float plane crossing the blue sky. He waved his arms and splashed.

But McCormick, Katherine, Silas, and their pilot, Jeremy Cooper, could not see the fjord hidden behind the steep cliffs.

"Could we follow the coastline on the way south for a few miles?" McCormick asked.

Cooper nodded, glad to help. "Follow it all the way to Mexico, if you like."

McCormick managed a weak smile of gratitude before turning his attention back out the window. Green ocean, black rock, craggy coast, green forest, and more and more of the same.

On the ground below, Angus scrambled to the base of the nearest cliff and screamed at the top of his lungs.

"WAIT! HELP! HELLLP!"

The scream shriveled into sobs as the plane flew away. "Wait... please ... I'm here ..."

Yellow Dog caught up to Angus and nudged his nose under the boy's hand. Angus pushed the dog away roughly.

It was too awful. The plane had been right there! Angus' heart pumped with wild irrational rage.

Yellow Dog's comforting gestures meant nothing to him. There was no room for anything but anger. THE PLANE WAS GONE!

Angus picked up a stick and swung it at the dog. Yellow Dog ducked in time to avoid the blow. Angus smashed the stick against the rocky cliff until it broke into splinters. Then he fell on his knees and cried — loud, choking, hysterical sobs from the bottom of his aching stomach.

Yellow Dog slinked closer to Angus, hoping the boy's anger had been exhausted.

Angus heard the dog approach. Still needing to strike out at someone, he snatched up a handful of pebbles and hurled them at Yellow Dog. Even through his thick yellow fur, the pebbles stung.

Yellow Dog sprinted about fifty feet from Angus, then lay down in confusion with his head between his paws. He watched the boy cry for a few minutes, before backing away from the fjord and out of sight.

CHAPTER

11

ngus sobbed until his eyes felt too dry to cry. The plane was gone. There was nothing he could do now but keep on walking, or give up. And he wasn't ready to give up . . . yet.

Before long, Angus stood between a rock and a green place. The only way he could keep going south would be to walk through the dense forest or over a steep rock cliff.

The boy sank to his knees and dropped his head down. Yellow Dog, who had never been far away, came up and pushed his muzzle against Angus. He started to lick the tears off the boy's cheeks, but Angus pushed him away hard.

"Get away!" Angus cried. "Get out of here!"

Then he pushed the dog again. Finally, Yellow Dog slinked away.

Angus clambered up the rocks and continued south, but soon hit another dead end. If all fifteen miles were going to be like this, the boy realized he might never reach the lighthouse.

He sat down and blew on the silver whistle. His anger was gone, and he felt ashamed of what he had done to the dog. "Here boy. Yellow," Angus called.

But for once, there was no eager trot, no wagging tail in response to the whistle's clear tone. Instead, Angus found himself eye-to-yellow eye with a wolf. The wild creature stared at the boy, then lifted its lips in a snarl.

Angus saw the fringe of sharp white teeth and imagined them sinking into his arm. His whole body shook with fear as he fumbled for a rock at his feet. Angus threw the rock at the wolf, who ambled off.

As he picked his way over the rocky terrain, the boy kept a sharp eye out for wolves. He never lost the sense that eyes were watching him with a terrible, persistent patience.

Whenever his fear abated, Angus' loneliness returned in full force. Finally, he sat at the edge of the forest and blew the silver whistle again. Then he looked anxiously up and down the shore.

Yellow Dog's tail hung down between his legs as he slinked up toward Angus. Tears of joy welled in the boy's eyes. The dog had come back!

"Good dog!" Angus exclaimed. "Good boy."

The dog's tail sprang up and wagged as Angus squeezed him in a tight hug.

That night, boy and dog huddled in a hastily built driftwood shelter near the forest's edge. Rain splattered on the logs and found its way between them. A tiny fire spluttered and smoked feebly, as Angus cooked part of a packet of instant soup, mixed with mussels and seaweed.

The rain grew heavier and the fire died. Yellow Dog suddenly stepped outside the shelter and barked. Angus peeked out and saw two wolves about thirty feet away. He pulled Yellow Dog back inside.

Lighting flashed and Angus saw the terrifying form of the wolves in stark silhouette. Once more the patient predators ambled away. But Angus knew they would not go far.

As the storm raged on, Angus and Yellow Dog huddled in their feeble shelter. Angus barely heard a faint snarl over the din of rain and wind. But Yellow Dog heard it well and lunged out of the shelter to jump at the lone wolf.

The wolf ran, and Yellow Dog ran after it up the dark beach. Another wolf appeared at the shelter. Angus felt too afraid to move. His terrified eyes stared back at the forest. Should he try it? Could he make it?

Angus shuddered. The wolves would surely follow him. And they could certainly run faster than him through the woods at night.

Lightning crackled over the forest, followed by an angry boom of thunder. In the flash of light, Angus saw twisted black branches like the arms of death itself. He shrank deeper in his shelter and fumbled for his knife.

The blade shook in Angus' hand as he waved it at the wolf. The creature was not at all impressed, but growled and jumped at the side of the shelter. Its snarling face glared at Angus through the slats.

The boy snatched up a piece of wood and hammered it at the wolf. "Stay back! Get away! YELLOW DOG!"

The wolf advanced on Angus, who was so frozen with

fear that he couldn't even close his eyes against the terrible vision. Suddenly, Yellow Dog threw himself into the fray! The loyal Labrador knocked the wolf sideways.

Then Yellow Dog stood between the wolf and Angus and snarled with a fury even more terrible than the wolf's. Yellow Dog's rumbling growl made one thing quite clear: he would die for Angus — and the wolf would die too.

The wolf turned tail and ran. Yellow Dog chased it a little way, then returned.

Angus had read about people being "frozen with fear." But he had never known the sensation before, except in nightmares. Even the sound of wolf howls growing nearer as the pack closed in couldn't shock the boy into movement.

Yellow Dog looked at Angus, then ran into the forest. He barked urgently. The boy knew what the dog meant. *Come on! What are you waiting for?*

But Angus had lost the will to fight. He was cold, hungry, exhausted, and scared out of his wits. He hugged his knees to his chest and tried to be too small to notice.

Yellow Dog barked again. He trotted back to Angus, then back to the forest. But the boy was motionless. Yellow Dog returned to the woods alone.

Slowly, Angus ripped a piece off his shirt and tied it to a stick. His shaking hands managed to ignite the makeshift torch, but its light barely reached beyond his hand and face.

Tears mixed with the rain on Angus' cheeks. Thunder shook him to his core as he forced one foot in front of the other toward the black forest. The boy's legs felt like lead, but he was not yet ready to die, so he walked.

The sound of snarling made Angus look over his shoulder. There were the wolves gathered on the beach. As Angus stepped into the dark embrace of the forest, the tiny light of his torch winked out.

Under the thick canopy of trees, the rain was more bearable. But the darkness was so complete, Angus crawled with his arms held out before him like a blind man. Hot tears drenched the boy's cheeks. His shaking fingers reached into the terrible blackness for something, anything!

Angus felt something warm beneath his left arm: fur and muscle, and the nudge of a friendly muzzle. Yellow Dog was with him! And he guided Angus through the darkness like a Seeing Eye dog.

The next morning, Angus made another marker on the beach, this time of driftwood and rocks. He arranged three pieces of driftwood to form an arrow pointing into the forest. Now Yellow Dog was happy to follow. This direction made more sense to him than traveling south.

"There's nowhere to go now," Angus explained. "We have to go through the trees. There might be a farm over the mountain, right?"

Yellow Dog wagged his tail.

Somehow, having survived that terrible night of wolves and darkness, Angus felt better. He told the dog as they clambered up a mossy hill, "Nothing's impossible, Yellow, just more difficult."

His parents kept telling themselves that too. Though it seemed impossible that Angus was still alive, they did not want to give up the search.

"We want to go back once, just to look, just to see if there's anything or anyplace we missed," Katherine told the dozen or so volunteers gathered in the farmhouse kitchen.

"I can't speak for all of us," one replied. "But for me, I can go right away, wherever you want."

Katherine's heart was full of gratitude as she heard the clamor of agreement.

David and Silas heard the sound of the adults talking, but they didn't pay attention. They were in Angus and Silas' bedroom. David played with a video game, while Silas held the old compass and studied Angus' rumpled chart.

"If he had this, he'd know where to go," Silas said.

David tried to make the little boy feel better, "Yeah, but it's okay that he doesn't because you can look at the sun and tell where you are, anyway."

Silas smiled. "Yeah, Angus is pretty smart."

David felt the emptiness in the room, but tried to sound cheerful. "Yeah, Angus is pretty smart."

"So's Yellow," Silas said. Then he looked at the wiggling line of the compass and felt sure he knew where Angus was going.

Just then, McCormick came into the room with a plate of sandwiches. "Here's some food, you guys."

"He's going west now, Dad," Silas reported.

McCormick smiled. There was something touching in Silas' complete belief. It was absurd, yet somehow convincing.

McCormick knelt down beside Silas and looked at the chart. Silas tapped the compass again. The needle pointed just south of west. "See," Silas said.

Silas handed his father the compass just before McCormick boarded the float plane. "Here, Dad, you'll need this. Angus said I could find out where he was just by checking it."

McCormick held the compass, then passed it back to Silas. "You know what? You better keep it so you know where we both are, okay?"

Silas nodded. "Yeah, I'd better, Dad."

McCormick folded Katherine and Silas in a tight hug.

"See you in a few days," Katherine said, trying hard not to cry.

While his father hunted for him, Angus hunted for mice. The trap was a propped-up cage of woven twigs connected to a fishing line. The bait was a piece of one of Sara's cookies.

Angus had waited so long for a mouse to appear that he had fallen asleep with the fishing line still clutched in his hand. Yellow Dog saw two mice nibbling the bait and nudged Angus awake.

The boy tugged the line and the trap fell over one hapless mouse. "Gotcha!" Angus cried triumphantly. The mouse squeaked and nipped Angus' finger.

"Ow!" Angus snatched up his pack. He dumped the mouse in his cook pot and slammed on the lid. The pot rattled noisily as the mouse bounced off its walls.

Yellow Dog and Angus drank greedily from a pond. Then Angus held the cooking pot toward the water. Yellow Dog whined. "I know it's an animal, but we need to do this," Angus explained. The dog watched silently as Angus filled the pot with water.

He drooled hungrily when Angus roasted the mouse on a stick over a tiny flame. Angus slid the small carcass off the skewer. Having been so close to death himself, he could not help feeling sorry for the creature.

"Thank you for being here to feed us, mouse." Angus looked around the forest. "Now you're with the wind and the stars and the trees where all the animal spirits go."

Yellow Dog looked at Angus. The boy's scratched skin barely covered his bones. Dark circles surrounded his haunted eyes. Boy and dog ate their meager meal in silence.

While Angus licked his fingers, his father read the sign written in charcoal on the red boat's oar. McCormick turned to the other searchers and said, "He went along the shore. Good boy."

But Angus wasn't walking along the shore anymore. He was deep in the forest, which was alive with birds and animals who stared curiously at the strange creature.

"Are we going the right way?" Angus asked. He was dizzy from hunger and exhaustion and the endless passing parade of tangled green. "I mean, are we going back the way we came or . . . or what? I don't know, Yellow."

Angus looked up through the treetops and found the sun. Now he knew which way was west, but Angus still felt completely lost.

"I think you should lead, Yellow," Angus said. "You've got six senses. I only have five."

An idea suddenly struck the boy. "Can you go home?

Can you find home, Yellow? Go on, go home Yellow!"

Yellow Dog snapped to attention. His ears perked up, his tail wagged. Home! Yellow Dog circled Angus, staying close at the boy's left side. Then he started forward at a brisk trot. Yellow Dog looked back and barked, and Angus followed.

Later, while they rested under a canopy of cedar trees, Angus used his grandfather's knife to make shin guards out of loose bark and a hood from a piece of his tarp. The shin guards kept his legs from getting even more scratched, and the hood helped a little against the rain.

Soon, boy and dog were up and walking again. Angus examined the notches on his "calendar." "The stick says we've been out eleven days, but I think I might have cut one day twice. I forget. Do you know, Yellow? Bark once for each day if you know."

Yellow Dog barked once.

Angus chuckled to himself, even though he was breathless from climbing up steep slopes. "Only one day. I feel much better now."

CHAPTER

12

 hat evening, Angus and Yellow Dog sheltered in a crevice in a rock wall. They huddled under the tattered tarp and watched rain pour over the rocks outside. The boy warmed his hands over a tiny fire.

Angus soaked one of Sara's cookies in a cup of water. Despite the wretched taste, he ate some of the crumbly mush. Yellow Dog did too.

"Do you think we're starving?" Angus asked, as he cleaned his knife.

Yellow Dog lay his head down in the boy's lap.

"Me too." Angus patted the soft yellow fur. "You could just take off. Why don't you? You could be a wild dog and join the wolves, and then you guys could hunt deer or whatever. You'd have meat for days."

Angus' stomach growled. "I'm making myself more hungry." When he spoke again, his tone was serious. "If I die, would you eat me?"

The tiny firelight gleamed on the knife blade. Yellow Dog whined.

"Huh? *No way.* I could never kill you, Yellow," Angus assured the dog. "I love you too much." Angus felt a lump grow in his throat. His eyes misted with tears. "I wonder where Dad is. You think they found him at least? Yeah, probably, huh? He's bigger, easier to see from a plane. I hope he's okay. I know he's okay."

Yellow Dog stopped listening to Angus. He bolted upright. The fur on his neck bristled and his lips parted in an angry growl. Was there something in the woods?

The following morning, John Gale and the McCormicks drank coffee in a cheery diner. But their mood was far from cheerful.

"Fifteen days is a long time. It's been eight since we started on land. Predators won't be very hungry right at the moment, but it hasn't been great weather this summer," Gale said. Facts were facts and they had to be faced.

Yesterday search planes had flown over an ocean of trees so dense it probably would have been easier if the boy *was* lost at sea. On the ground, McCormick and several exhausted volunteers had clambered among the waves crashing on sea-worn stones. The searchers had found no further trace of Angus.

Gale studied his friend's worn face. Determination sparked in McCormick's blue eyes. "He's really good in the bush," McCormick asserted.

Katherine agreed. "McCormick taught him all kinds of survival techniques."

Gale could see that his friends were not ready to give up on their son — and he couldn't blame them. Still, they had to accept the reality of the situation. "We don't actually know he went inland," Gale began.

Electric Shock Man suddenly piped up. "Yes we do, the compass says so," Silas said with deep conviction.

"Silas," Katherine warned.

McCormick looked Gale in the eyes. "How long will you keep going?"

"As long as there is a reasonable expectation . . ."

Katherine cut off Gale's reply. "Then we've got a reasonable expectation that you'll keep looking for a long time."

Gale sensed the mother lion in Katherine's sharp tone. McCormick tried to keep the discussion calm. "He's not saying they're . . ."

Katherine snapped, "They *are not* going to stop looking!"

Gale said hastily, "I didn't say that. Look, I'm sorry. Very often we can't find entire aircraft down in the trees. I mean, eventually we find them, but . . . well, you know."

Katherine's eyes blazed. Gale realized he'd just thrown gasoline on a fire. "Come with me for a couple of hours. I'll show you what I mean."

In the dense thicket of trees, crows cawed over clattering bones. Yellow Dog snapped at one of the big black birds that came too close to the thigh bone he gnawed. Angus woke up and realized he was surrounded by deer bones picked clean by birds. In the dark he had not realized that their shelter was a burial ground where

99

sick and wounded deer came to die. The rain had stopped, but a low mist hugged the cold ground. Ferns dripped with sparkling moisture.

Angus crushed one of Sara's cookies against a rock and mixed it with water and a handful of roots and berries. He scooped the mash into his mouth with bony fingers, then put the lid carefully back on the cookie tin.

While he mechanically chewed and swallowed the bitter mixture, Angus heard the distant drone of a plane engine. He looked up, but saw only branches and sunlight. Angus knew if he couldn't see the plane, there was no hope the plane could see him.

"We're never going to get out of here. Are we, Yellow?" the boy said in despair. He scooped another handful of mush and held it out to the dog. But Yellow Dog preferred his bone.

The plane was a mile distant. It was a de Havilland DHC-5 Buffalo, a brown cargo carrier emblazoned with a red maple leaf. Katherine stared out one of the plane's windows at the solid sea of trees. She saw a mountain, a valley with a lake, hills, another mountain top. And all were covered in green, green, green. Now she understood why Gale had his doubts about whether they could ever find Angus. She felt too sad even to cry.

Angus carved notch number sixteen on his stick while Yellow Dog sucked the marrow from another bone. Angus warmed his hands over a tiny flame. "A turkey dinner with pies and cakes and a gallon of ice cream, and maybe a couple of orders of fries with lots of salt," the boy said dreamily.

Hunger sent Angus to a nearby river. He tied Yellow Dog to a tree on the bank, then waded into the frigid water. The boy stood, feet numb and teeth chattering. His hand clutched a sharpened stick as he peered through bright reflections, watching for fish shadows. Dad had taught him that most fish had protective coloring, but you could always spot their shadows. Yellow Dog strained at his rope. He wanted to go fishing too.

Angus stabbed at a shadow slithering through the water. His spear struck the rocky bed. Disappointment washed over him, but he tried again. This time his spear struck a fish. He felt it struggle for a moment, before he carefully carried it to the bank.

When the fish stopped flopping, Angus smashed its head with a stone. As a quick reward, he cut a piece of the raw flesh and popped it in his mouth. Then he went back to the water to catch more.

By afternoon, rain was falling as it so often does in the Pacific Northwest. Angus and Yellow Dog found shelter in a dirt cave beneath the roots of a fallen tree. Angus cooked a mash of fish, berries, and crumbled cookies over a small fire. He held some of the warm mash out to Yellow Dog.

"No more food. No more matches," Angus reported sadly. He pulled his fingers out of the dog's snapping jaws. "Take it easy with my fingers."

Angus and Yellow Dog heard a low grunt over the rush of the rain and the crackling of the fire. Yellow Dog barked as a big brown paw reached into the cave.

Angus was stunned. A bear!

Suddenly the big furry owner of the brown paw filled

101

the entrance to the cave. Fat with summer feasting, the bear had grown almost too big for his den. He squeezed into the tight entrance, determined to claim his dry home. His rude visitors barked and poked a burning stick at him. Then the bear was showered with rocks and dirt.

Angus threw rocks from a relatively safe distance. But Yellow Dog bravely confronted the furious bear. Angus cringed as big curved claws swatted inches away from Yellow Dog's chest.

Angus pawed the ground desperately. He had run out of rocks! So he grabbed one of Sara's cookies and pitched it at the angry beast. By chance, Angus struck the bear on its tender nose. The bear roared in pain and backed out of the cave.

The bear swatted at the offending missile. He flipped the cookie into his mouth. To the huge bruin, it tasted good!

There was no accounting for taste, Angus thought. The bear came back to the cave for more!

Angus pitched the entire tin outside. The bear chomped it between his giant jaws, then dragged the tin away. He shook open his treasure and gulped down the sweet contents. Satisfied, the bear lumbered off into the rain.

Angus sighed. "Thanks, Sara."

His friend wasn't much of a cook, but, in an indirect way, she had saved his life. Angus remembered that moment on the dock when they had almost kissed. If he had that chance again, he would not hesitate!

CHAPTER

13

he day the orcas came that summer, the old man died,'" Katherine read aloud from *Waiting for the Whales*. She sat with Silas on his cot in their room at the Blue Vista Motel, wishing she had found a more cheerful bedtime story.

"Would you go to space or maybe under the ocean when you die?" Silas asked.

"Um . . ." Katherine wasn't in the mood for one of those impossible questions kids will always throw your way. But she knew she couldn't duck out of this one, not now. "Well, you go to heaven . . . maybe, but probably." Recent events had made her faith a bit shaky.

"And then you open your eyes and wake up again," Silas stated.

"No, you don't open your eyes again. It's like sleep, but different." Katherine wondered what she was getting into.

"It's forever?" Silas persisted.

Katherine sighed. "Yes, it is."

"Well, at least you can go visit people whenever you want. That's something, maybe," Silas suggested.

Tears sprang to Katherine's bloodshot eyes.

"You shouldn't worry too much, you know," Silas said.

Not knowing what to say, Katherine hugged him.

Inside the fish-plant office, Gale wondered, "How far do you think he'd get inland — a mile a day?"

He sat across from McCormick at a table cluttered with maps and charts. Gale had drawn a circle around the place where an army search party had found the remains of Angus' last beach camp and the driftwood arrow pointing into the forest.

McCormick looked at the circle and shook his head. "More than that. Twice that."

Gale nodded and made a wider circle on the map. The search had a focus now, even if Gale was highly skeptical that the boy had survived the seventeen days. But at least they had some idea where to look.

McCormick went back to the motel room and persuaded Katherine to go home. He would stay with Gale until the end — one way or the other.

"I'll find him," McCormick declared.

Katherine did not want to leave, but she relented. For Silas' sake, she would go home. "You need to explain heaven to Silas," said Katherine. "He doesn't understand."

The next morning, Silas was dressed as an ordinary little boy, not Electric Shock Man or Meteor Boy. But he still hugged his old compass. John Gale loaded the

McCormicks' luggage into Jeremy Cooper's float plane.

"I'll call every day," McCormick promised Katherine.

Silas tugged at his father's pant leg. "You can use the compass now, Dad."

This time McCormick accepted the boy's gift. He hugged Silas and said, "I will. It'll find him. Take care of Mom, okay?"

Jeremy Cooper didn't mind taking the long way back to Saturna Island. He would have flown all the way to the Atlantic coast if it would have helped Katherine find her boy.

At that moment, Angus was contemplating his breakfast wriggling in the palm of his hand: a live worm, a dead bee, a wood beetle, and a moth larva. His fingers were crusted with dirt from digging his meal out of the ground. Angus tossed the bugs in his pot and added a trickle of water.

"Finest source of protein on the planet," Angus said in a voice that sounded like McCormick's. "Fat and stuff too."

Yellow Dog looked at the mush in the pot and snorted disapprovingly. Angus wondered if the dog was right, but decided to stick with his father's advice. "If *I've* got to, *you've* got to," he told Yellow Dog.

While the dog made a disgusted face, Angus held his nose and ate. Angus' hollow eyes widened in surprise at the nutty flavor. "Not bad." He held the pot out to Yellow Dog once more. "Here, have some."

He scooped out a handful of the glop and coaxed, "Yellow, Yellow, you've got to . . ."

But the dog turned and walked stiffly away. Angus chased after him, trying to blow the whistle, but it sounded only a faint twitter.

105

Angus followed the dog up a steep trail. His legs felt like jelly. The boy collapsed on a log.

Yellow Dog looked back and barked. But Angus couldn't go on. "I'm just resting . . . for a minute. I get tired too fast now. I've only got two fee—"

Angus stopped in mid-word at the sound of an engine. High above, Jeremy Cooper's float plane crossed the green island. Angus couldn't see the plane, but he noticed something glinting on the top of a nearby hill. Yellow Dog barked.

"You want to go that way?" Angus asked. "Okay. Nobody's looking for us up here anyway, right? Let's go."

Angus stood up so quickly the blood never reached his head. The trees spun around him just before his eyes closed in a faint. The boy rolled off the trail and down the steep slope, sliding 300 feet to the bottom of the hill.

Angus woke to find Yellow Dog licking his wounds. The boy sat up and almost fainted again, this time from pain. Angus saw a lump rising on his right wrist. He knew what that meant. And with the knowledge, the pain came in earnest. The boy's scream echoed off the lonely cliff. His wrist was broken!

Once the scream stopped echoing, Angus pulled himself together. He remembered what his father had taught him about broken bones. He knew what to do. Now if only he could do it!

Angus found a stump with a wedge rotted out of the middle. He crawled to it and set his wrist in the empty wedge. He braced a foot on either side of the stump and took a deep breath. "One . . . two . . . three . . ."

Angus leaned back with all his might. With a sickening crunch, the broken bone snapped back into place. After one agonized wail, Angus again fainted.

Later, the boy splinted his arm and used his sleeve to make a sling. Yellow Dog watched him, concerned.

"I'm okay, Yellow," Angus said bravely. "Hurts though."

Yellow Dog licked the boy's face. Angus climbed to his feet, and they set off toward the distant valley together. Angus chatted, and Yellow Dog listened.

Their progress toward the glint on the mountain was painfully slow. The forest opened up, and they found themselves in the tangled undergrowth on the beach of a large lake. Angus dropped to his knees on the rocky beach.

"How are we going to do this now, Yellow?" the boy wondered. Yellow Dog flopped on the shore. Angus shrugged. "I guess we'll just do it."

Working with only one arm, Angus spent the whole day binding three small logs with the yellow nylon rope. At last he had a raft.

Angus and Yellow Dog launched their shaky vessel. Angus struggled to paddle with one tired arm. Yellow Dog swam in front, pulling the raft with the rope tied to his collar. "If they flew over right now, they'd see something, right?" Angus asked, as he stared up into the clear blue sky.

Yellow Dog swam on without answering. Angus stopped paddling and curled into a ball on the rocking raft. His arm was black and blue and swollen.

Trying to keep dry, Angus turned. But he lost his balance on the shaky raft and rolled into the freezing water.

107

Yellow Dog nudged Angus under the arm, pushing the boy up to the surface. Angus clutched the raft, coughing. Cold water and fear made him shiver. "I can't get back up, Yellow," the boy confessed.

Yellow Dog growled. Angus kicked, pushing the raft while the dog pulled. Somehow they made it to the other shore. Angus fell asleep almost the moment his soggy body touched land.

A big black raven swooped down out of the sky and eyed the boy. Yellow Dog sneaked up on the bird, then suddenly barked. Yellow Dog was satisfied when the bird flapped frantically back into the sky. He barked again, just to be sure.

The sound drowned out McCormick's voice as he shouted into the forest miles away. "ANGUS! ANGUS!" McCormick cried. But the only reply was the screech of an eagle and the cawing of crows.

McCormick slumped on a fallen tree with his head in his hands. The forest was so huge. Angus was so small. And McCormick could never shake the feeling that it was all his fault.

"We'd better get going, Mr. McCormick," one of the ground search volunteers said gently.

"Good dog!" Angus croaked. He was hiding in a huge cedar stump twenty feet across, that must have been cut down a hundred years ago.

Yellow Dog had stolen a small deer carcass from a lynx. The wildcat had fought back furiously, but Yellow Dog held it at bay. The big cat's long pointed ears flattened against its hissing head. Angus pitched rocks until the speckled beast finally bounded into the woods.

Boy and dog feasted on raw venison. "It's a little one, Yellow, still warm even. How did you steal it like that? We could eat for weeks." Angus wished he had matches, so he could cook the meat. But maybe with enough sunshine, he could pound it, mix it with fat, and dry it into pemmican balls like Dad had taught him. That was real wilderness food.

If they could catch more meat, Angus would grow strong. He could set traps. If they weren't going to find him, maybe Angus could survive on his own. He'd just have to find a cave and get up a good store of dry wood. Then his thoughts stopped. He wasn't ready to become a wild man.

"You think they're still looking for us?" he asked.

Yellow Dog belched.

"How long do you think they'll keep looking?" Angus wondered. The dog whined, and Angus said, "That's what I think. We've got to get across that valley tomorrow, Yellow. We've got to! People haven't been here for a hundred years, and I don't think they'll be back real soon."

The searchers came back to the old fish cannery headquarters with the last light of day. Gale sensed that McCormick was almost too tired to go on, but he knew his friend wouldn't give up.

"Okay, let's try putting everything we've got over land," Gale suggested to Alan Smith, a Coast Guard officer.

"We've got a huge grid covered already," Smith replied. "We can't go much bigger."

The ground search leader added, "We might get about five or six more planes up this week, but that's just five or

109

six more planes trying to see through canopy. We need more ground search teams."

Smith wondered if all the time and expense were being wasted. Disasters were not uncommon. You couldn't put all your resources into each one or you wouldn't be ready for the next. "Seventeen days is a long time, John. I'm not certain —"

Gale interrupted, "Yeah, well, *I'm* certain. We didn't find the boy or the dog. But we found two encampments and it looks a lot like he went inland. He's a tough kid."

Smith could see Gale was as stubborn as the kid's father. And what if they were right? "We'll expand the grid for three days, then try and get everyone out without some disaster happening . . ."

"The disaster already happened!" Gale exclaimed. "How can we move more people inland?"

"We have to fly in some more helicopters," said Smith.

"Fly them in then," Gale ordered. "Have them here in the morning."

Gale turned on his heel and hurried to the end of the dock where McCormick was boarding Cooper's float plane. "I've got another few planes for tomorrow," Gale reported.

"That's great. Thanks, John. I'll be back in three days, four at the most," McCormick said vaguely. He'd been living on coffee and hope for too long to think clearly. He didn't want to leave at all, but he had to. "Insurance, business, other stuff . . . all kinds of things." He'd left Katherine holding the bag long enough, but nothing seemed to matter except finding Angus.

"Don't worry," Gale said. Then he added ruefully. "Know

what? Worry all you want. I would. I'm stretching the search two more hours after daylight. Maybe we'll spot a little campfire or something. I'll have a plane waiting for you when you're ready to come back."

McCormick shifted Silas' compass to his left hand so he could shake Gale's with his right. "Couple of days, that's all," he said. But the days lately were awfully long,

14

ime passed slowly for Angus as well. He marked off another day on his calendar stick. The morning sun found him scrambling up a steep rock slide. Rough deer-hide sandals covered Angus' sore feet. The massive boulders lay like building blocks scattered by some careless giant child. They were heaped between a sheer rock wall and the forest.

"You'd better be right about the direction you've chosen," Angus said.

Later, they came to a rotting wooden ladder nailed to the legs of an abandoned fire lookout tower. Angus climbed slowly. His broken wrist ached. "When we're above the trees, we'll see where we are. We'll see a way out."

Angus pushed open the creaking door. A dozen birds flew out of broken windows, angry at the sudden intrusion. A century of peace had descended on the place since the loggers had left.

The boy examined the small square room. Pine needles, sticks, dirt, moss, and debris littered the floor and the few simple shelves. A rusted woodstove squatted in the center. Angus looked out all the windows, then stopped at one facing a long valley. There was a road! And a wisp of smoke! People! There were people alive in the world, and not so very far away! Angus stared at the wonderful sight.

"We'll cross the valley to the road now," he said.

Below him, Yellow Dog flopped down into a puddle of tawny fur.

"Good dog," Angus said. "Are you hungry? We'd better eat something because I'm too tired to walk anymore."

Angus slumped in the corner and closed his eyes. He was asleep in seconds.

McCormick was making a snack for himself in the farmhouse's quiet kitchen. "I have to go to the insurance people again tomorrow," he said as he smeared jelly on the peanut butter sandwich.

"Silas, hold still," Katherine commanded. "Let me match the seam." Silas fidgeted on a kitchen chair while Katherine hemmed the legs of his new pants. School would be starting again soon. He couldn't dress like a superhero there.

"They'll let us have the whole value of the boat, but there's an argument about the cargo," McCormick said.

There was a quiver in Katherine's voice when she replied. "Tell them you can't put a value on what was on the boat."

Silas knew, they all knew, what she was refering to. But all Katherine said was, "Did you talk to the school?"

"How about in a few days?" McCormick said quietly. Because talking to the school meant admitting that Angus would not be attending. Then the loss would be even more painfully real.

"Hold still, Si," Katherine said.

A long, uncomfortable silence filled the room. Then McCormick said, "I'm going to work on the truck."

Silas joined his father in the tractor shed. He leaned over the fender, the way McCormick did. Silas stared into the maze of tubes, wires, and metal shapes. The smell of gasoline and stale oil filled his nostrils.

"Now we unscrew the spark plugs," McCormick began. "Hold them for me, okay?"

Silas took the oily spark plugs in his small hands. He had seen Angus work with their dad, and now he was. "Angus and Yellow aren't going to come back, are they?" Silas spoke the truth that no one else dared to say.

McCormick looked at his son, but could not answer.

Angus only meant to sleep for a few minutes, but he woke up fifteen hours later, dazed and confused. He blinked in the sunlight, which came from a surprising direction. When he had fallen asleep the sun was shining on the other side of the tower. He was alone. "Yellow? Yellow Dog? Here boy," Angus called.

Then he blew the silver whistle and waited. A bark answered from outside. Angus pulled himself to his feet. He saw Yellow Dog not far from the tower. The dog barked, and Angus climbed down and followed him into the trees.

As they walked, he foraged like an ape, crawling around

tree roots, plucking berries, and scraping lichen off bark. The sunlight became patchy, as clouds gathered over the canopy of trees. It was going to rain, of course. Angus was accustomed to that.

By following a trail of ants, Angus found water cupped in the hollow of a tree. Dad had told him ants and bees were never far from fresh water. As Angus scooped some water to his mouth, Yellow Dog popped out of the underbrush with a rabbit wriggling in his jaws.

Angus thought *food*. He took the rabbit from the dog and killed it with a stick. This time he did not hesitate. He was not the same boy who spared the hare on the cliff.

Angus felt a lot better after eating the rabbit. He gave a loud burp, which was answered by one from Yellow Dog. Angus laughed with the simple joy of a full stomach.

Angus and Yellow Dog had left the fire tower far behind. Dark clouds filled the sky. The rain would come soon now, but Angus could not let that stop him. When the trees parted, they found themselves at the edge of a canyon.

Below, a rushing river roared and gurgled. The water writhed like a silver snake between the steep granite cliffs. Angus looked up and down the gorge. They could not walk around the river. They would have to cross it. And they would have to cross it now, before the rain trapped them without shelter.

Two dead trees spanned the hundred-and-fifty-foot gap between the cliffs. This natural bridge was the only way across. Yellow Dog whined. Angus kneeled down next to him. "You helped me across the lake. I'll help you across the logs."

The dog did not like the idea at all. Angus thought the

only way to get Yellow Dog to cross would be if he went first. "Come on, it's okay. It's easy!" the boy fibbed. Walking across the trees wasn't hard exactly, unless you looked down!

Angus grabbed a branch to steady himself. The dry wood snapped with a loud CRACK. Angus sat down fast to keep himself from falling. "Just don't grab rotten branches," Angus advised the dog.

The desire to be with Angus overcame Yellow Dog's fear of heights. He inched onto the log bridge. His head hung low between his shoulders, and his yellow brow was furrowed with worry. A slow steady whine came with each breath.

The grumbling clouds swirled in a rising wind. Angus felt the first drops of rain spatter on his skin. Soon, drops pelted his face. The wind pushed and tugged at him as if it was trying to make him fall. Angus slid across the suddenly slippery bark.

The boy took another step toward the far cliff, and the tree cracked! There was no turning back now. If Angus and Yellow didn't reach the other side soon . . . Angus crawled frantically as the wind howled around him. Branches whipped around him and tore at his pack.

Angus was stuck. He had to take off the pack. But when he did, the wind grabbed it and whipped it open. The boy watched helplessly as his coat, mess kit, and all he owned fell into the raging river. Everything was gone, even the silver whistle.

All Angus managed to save was the tarp, which nearly pulled him off the log with its wild flapping. He managed to pull the cloth over himself and the dog. "When it stops raining, we'll go back, okay dog?" Angus soothed the shivering beast.

Above the sound of the storm, the boy heard a steady, mechanical drone. At first he was reluctant to believe his ears, to have hope rise only to be dashed again. But then he saw a plane flying right up the canyon.

With his good arm, Angus waved the tarp. He waved and waved, never sure if the tiny plane saw him. And then the plane was gone. Angus put his face down on the mossy log. "Good-bye, plane."

There was only the sound of the rain and the river and the wind. Angus was alone in the forest with Yellow Dog, and the old watch tower, and the eagles, rabbits, and deer. *This is the way it would always be,* he thought. The forest would close in over him, and all the people he loved would never even know where he'd been, like a pebble tossed into a deep lake. The ripples would fade very fast.

And then the bright red-and-yellow plane roared over the gorge. The bridge shook. Angus was almost too terrified and astonished to feel joy or relief. His ears rang with the engine's deafening hum. "They came back!"

The plane banked and turned, then came back again. It was true! Angus could hardly believe it after all this time. The plane had seen him! The plane was coming back for him! He was ... going home!

"Search master," John Gale answered the phone at the cannery. He was just as amazed as Angus. Gale slammed down the receiver and ran from the office, yelling at the top of his lungs. "They found him! They found him!"

"They found him! They found him!" Katherine screamed

117

as she ran from the farmhouse to the tractor shed. She jumped into McCormick's arms, and they slipped and fell in the mud. Then they picked each other up only to fall again. "Is he all right?" McCormick asked.

Katherine shrugged. "I don't know. Can we go now?"

Being found and being rescued were two different things. The storm was worse now. Wind and thunder almost drowned out the Labrador helicopter's heavy engines. Lightning crackled dangerously close to the whirring blades.

"He's about one mile east of the tower," Gale told the helicopter pilot, Jane Freeman.

Captain Freeman said, "I have the tower on the nose for two miles, steer 0-9-7."

Angus watched the huge helicopter hover directly over him. Bits of bark and dirt flew up in the swirling air churned by its rotors. The backwash ripped the tarp from his hand. The tarp fluttered like a wounded bird into the canyon.

Through the veil of his fingers, Angus peered at a black shape dropping like a spider from the noisy craft. John Gale watched the SARTECH swaying on his cable. This was a dangerous rescue. If the helicopter didn't crash, there were still a dozen other things that might go wrong.

"He's got a dog there with him," Gale pointed out.

"We've got a storm here with us," the pilot replied.

"Can't you just put a man down to walk out and get him?" Gale asked.

Jane Freeman didn't like the odds. "Tomorrow we can."

Gale couldn't bear the thought of leaving Angus now — not after searching for him for so long!

The man on the cable had no part in this debate. His job was to pick up that boy and try to keep from getting smashed against the log. At the moment, he was more likely to hit the log than reach the boy. He signaled for the cable to be raised. But the helicopter swung in the wind.

The SARTECH grabbed at the log to steady himself. The sudden movement excited Yellow Dog, who thought this strange being was attacking Angus.

Yellow Dog snapped and snarled. Angus tried to calm him. "It's okay boy, it's okay," Angus cooed. But Yellow Dog had never liked the sound of planes.

The SARTECH yelled over the rotor noise. "Reach over son. Are you okay?" And he reached out to Angus, who tottered in the SARTECH's direction.

Yellow Dog barked wildly. He wanted to run from the terrible noise, but he was trapped in this dreadful place high above the water.

The SARTECH swung away as the helicopter bounced on another gust of wind. Then, as he swung back, the SARTECH tried to pass a harness to Angus. The man managed to hook a leg over the log. He grabbed for the boy. He got his arms around Angus.

The winch whined as it pulled the cable upward. Yellow Dog went crazy. The flying creature was taking his friend up into the sky!

Without thought for his own safety, Yellow Dog lunged at the man. Four paws slipped off the log and fell through empty space. Angus saw Yellow Dog twisting in a futile attempt to right himself as he plunged toward the river.

Angus felt as if he were falling too. He didn't care that he was safe now on a stretcher inside the big helicopter.

Going home meant nothing if Yellow Dog couldn't come too.

"Mr. Gale, you've got to get my dog!" Angus pleaded with more strength than he had.

"It's okay, Angus. We'll get your dog," Gale promised the pale, skeletal face he could barely recognize as McCormick's older son.

Jane Freeman sighed with relief as the helicopter pulled up and away from the canyon. The storm clouds closed around the aircraft and the forest was silent, except for the wind, the rain, and the rushing river.

CHAPTER

15

ou people, out of here!" a nurse shouted at the reporters who mobbed the hospital hall.

McCormick, Katherine, and Silas elbowed through the crowd to reach Angus' room. Katherine was devastated by the sight of her son all skin, bones, and bruises. I.V. tubes ran up his nose and into his wrist. Monitor wires were taped to his bony chest. Machines bleeped and winked all around him.

"Hi, Mom. Hi, Dad. Hi, Si," Angus said.

Silas rolled his eyes as their parents engulfed Angus in a huge hug.

"They're going to get Yellow now, Si. Don't worry," Angus said.

John Gale was trying to do just that. But the Coast Guard wasn't enthusiastic about committing resources to a search for a missing dog.

121

"I just changed the status," Gale thundered. "It's now a missing *person*. That dog saved that kid's life out there, and it's hungry and cold and lost and probably thinks it's been deserted. So get the units up there right now!"

Sara was waiting at the McCormick farm, leaning on her bike under the trees, trying hard to look casual. Mr. McCormick carried Silas to the house.

Angus went out to meet Sara. He wasn't quite skin and bones anymore, and his arm was in a bright white cast.

"Hi, Angus," Sara said.

"Hi, Sara," Angus replied.

"Are you hungry? Coming in?" Katherine asked. She couldn't wait to feed him.

"In a minute, Mom." Was he hungry? That word had a new meaning for Angus. He was happy to see Sara, but his eyes strayed to the woodpile where he'd first touched Yellow Dog. *They have to find him,* Angus thought. The dog would be back soon. He had to be!

"Are you going to be back at school right away?" Sara wondered.

School. There was still school. It seemed childish and pointless to Angus. What was he going to do? Write an essay on "How I spent my summer vacation"?

That night, Angus' mother gently tried to tell him that Yellow Dog had probably been killed in the fall. She wanted Angus to get on with his life.

Her arguments made sense. But Angus couldn't bear the idea of never seeing Yellow Dog again.

In the last days of summer vacation, Angus resigned himself to the loss. Dad plowed the fields under, as he always did in early fall. Angus played catch with Silas and David. But his heart wasn't in it.

One night, John Gale came by and explained to McCormick that a search like the one they'd conducted for Angus cost $200,000 a week. They couldn't justify spending that on a dog.

Katherine had never liked the dog, but when she heard how much Yellow Dog had done to save her son, she did what she could. Katherine transmitted a LOST DOG bulletin over her computer modem. Thousands of people read the notice, but no one had seen Yellow Dog.

Angus' teacher, Mrs. Atkins, tried to make a big deal out of his "heroic efforts." But the boy just blushed and said, "My dog saved me."

Poor Angus did wind up writing how he spent his summer vacation for the local newspaper. He didn't like the attention he received. But it didn't bother him too much that Sara thought he was a hero. And he was awfully glad to have the chance to thank her for those cookies, even though he hadn't eaten most of them.

"Well, one," Angus said. "That was good. I kind of lost the others, by mistake. They got taken."

"I'll make you some more," Sara volunteered eagerly.

"Oh, that's okay," Angus said. He didn't want to hurt Sara's feelings. But now that he wasn't starving, even the *thought* of those burnt hockey pucks was pretty miserable.

Sara said, "So, if you want to come over later, you can. Nobody wants to say it, but you are a hero, you know."

"My dog's the hero," said Angus.

"He is too." Sara brushed some dirt from Angus' face. He thought for a second they were going to kiss. But once again it didn't happen.

Angus never gave up on Yellow Dog. Late in October, he and Silas made 500 copies of the lost-dog flyer. The whole island was papered with them. Jeremy Cooper handed out the flyer on all his runs. John Gale distributed more.

"Do you think Mr. Gale hung the flyers in the right places?" Angus asked his father.

They were in the barn, steam-bending ribs for his new red boat. "Yup, all 500 of them," McCormick said.

"How long do you think it would take to walk home from where they found me?" Angus wondered.

"If you could walk through the forest?" McCormick asked.

"You know, part way, then maybe on roads." Angus had pictured it all over and over in his mind. Yellow Dog had pulled himself out of the river. Then he'd started walking, and someday he was going to walk right across the McCormicks' field. He had to!

"Maybe thirty or forty days if you were a smart person, or dog," McCormick replied cautiously.

"I guess that might be pretty hard to do," Angus conceded.

"Yes, it might be," McCormick agreed. "Plus you'd have to cross back over to the island. Six-mile stretch of ocean there."

There was a long silence while Angus digested this information and measured it against his fantasy. Sorrow welled up in Angus' chest and filled him to the brim. But he didn't cry. "He just didn't know, Dad. He was trying to protect me. He didn't know they were trying to save me. Maybe I should have tried to grab him. I could've hung on to him and pulled him up to me, or reached for his collar and . . ."

McCormick hugged his son. Angus said, "Labradors can swim really well — distance, I mean."

"No better water dog in the world," his father agreed.

Angus had trouble finishing his essay for Mrs. Atkins because he didn't know the end of the story. The teacher gave him an extension until Monday and advised the boy to get another dog. "A boy always needs a dog."

After school, Angus and Sara walked home. The cold air put a bloom on her cheeks and her shoulder brushed against his.

"What if some farmer got him?" Angus wondered.

"Then they'll take care of him," Sara said.

"Yeah, you're right."

"Mrs. Atkins is right," Sara said. "You have to have a dog."

"Yeah, you're right." But Yellow Dog was the only dog Angus wanted. He tried to avoid Sara's gaze.

"Are you okay?" she asked.

"Yeah, I'm okay," Angus mumbled.

Sara said, "Yeah, you're right. You *are* okay."

Angus wondered what she meant. Sara put her arm around him, and he put his around her. Then Sara leaned close and kissed him. They stopped at a crossroads. Angus swallowed. "The store's going to close."

"See you tomorrow," Sara said with a satisfied smile.

"Yeah, you will for sure," Angus replied. "Okay. Right."

Then he remembered the promise he'd made to himself back in the forest. And Angus kissed Sara.

"Are you sure you want this?" Ron Willick asked. The question snapped the boy out of a dreamy daze. Willick slid a huge bag of dog food over the counter. "You sure you don't want the smaller one, Angus?"

"No, sir. This one. The one with the whistle inside," Angus answered.

The boy lugged the bag home, tore it open, and dumped it on the porch. He pawed through the brown kibble until he found the silver whistle. The familiar beautiful tone echoed off the hills.

At dawn the next morning, Angus made his way to the woodpile. The blue horizon was fringed in fragile pink.

Angus knew he had to try, even though he felt sure it wouldn't work. If he didn't do it, he'd never be able to get over Yellow Dog. But he knew it was going to hurt, hurt as bad as setting his broken wrist on the stump.

Angus walked to the split-rail fence at the edge of the field. He lifted the whistle to his lips and made himself blow it. Then he called out, "Yellow Dog! Here, boy!"

He waited and waited, but nothing happened. Angus was going to blow the whistle once more, but tears filled his eyes and choked his throat. He just couldn't do it. Then he said the words he didn't want to say. "Good-bye, Yellow Dog."

The words floated across the sparkling field until they were swallowed up by the golden dawn. Angus turned away and trudged back to the house.

The boy heard something. Maybe it was just the wind.

But maybe something else. He lifted the whistle one last time and blew it, one last time.

The single clear note echoed off the hills. There was an answering bark. And then another!

Then Angus' legs were carrying him across the yard, over the fence and through the field. And there was Yellow Dog running to him! He was the most bedraggled, limping, happiest dog in the world because he was home!